TWO CENTURIES OF ECUMENISM

BY THE SAME AUTHOR

IN FRENCH

L'Angoisse de l'Unité (Bonne Presse) 1952

IN ENGLISH

Transiency and Permanence: The Nature of Theology according to St. Bonaventure (Franciscan Institute) 1954

The Catholic Approach to Protestantism (Harper, N.Y.) 1955

The Church, the Layman and the Modern World (Macmillan, N.Y.) 1959

Protestantism (Twentieth Century Encyclopedia of Catholicism, Hawthorn Books, N.Y.) 1959

Holy Writ or Holy Church: The Crisis of the Protestant Reformation (Harper, N.Y.) 1960

Protestant Hopes and the Catholic Responsibility (Fides, Notre Dame, Ind.) 1960

TWO CENTURIES
OF ECUMENISM

By GEORGE H. TAVARD

Translated by ROYCE W. HUGHES

GREENWOOD PRESS, PUBLISHERS
WESTPORT, CONNECTICUT

BX
1784
.T3813
1978

Library of Congress Cataloging in Publication Data

Tavard, Georges Henri, 1922-
   Two centuries of ecumenism.

   Translation of Petite histoire du mouvement oecumén-
ique.
   Reprint of the ed. published by Fides Publishers
Association, Notre Dame, Ind.
   Bibliography: p.
   1. Christian union--Catholic Church--History.
2. Ecumenical movement--History. I. Title.
[BX1784.T3813 1978]   282'.09   78-6449
ISBN 0-313-20490-X

CONTENTS

INTRODUCTION

The problem of ecumenism is the order of the day. The theologians who study it and the apostles who preach brotherhood among severed Christians are no longer isolated. Their number and the number of their publications on ecumenism have been noticeably on the increase for some years past. Moreover, His Holiness Pope John XXIII has unhesitatingly brought up the ecumenical question before Catholics. This is an added reason, if there be need of one, to study the problem at hand.

There are various ways of approaching ecumenism. It is evident that the theologian must bring himself up to date on the history and present state of Orthodox theology and Anglican or Protestant thought. The majority of the faithful are not capable of undertaking such a study. Due to lack of time, it is impossible for them to attempt an extensive and detailed inquiry. Even if they had the time and the inclination for it, it might be dangerous to let them read Protestant authors assiduously, because they have no specialized training. They can resort to prayer. This is excellent. But like any other prayer, prayer for Christian unity must be nourished with intellectual and spiritual food. We should know what we are praying for. We also ought to know why we pray in this particular way. To put it in other words, the desire for Christian unity, to whatever degree it may exist, requires some knowledge of the problems of ecumenism.

There are some good introductions to ecumenism on the market. Apart from a relatively old but very valuable work by Msgr. Charles Journet,[1] the excellent books of Fathers Maurice Villain,[2] Karl Adam,[3] Roger Aubert,[4] and Charles Boyer [5] should also be consulted. Highly technical studies are no longer lacking. Those of Fathers Yves Congar,[6] Charles Dumont,[7] Louis Bouyer,[8] and Bishop Gustave Thils [9] are well known. Altogether, these make up an impressive library, to which numerous titles can be added in time.

The list which might be drawn up contains a gap however. We still don't have a history of Catholic ecumenism. There are studies on one aspect or another of the ecumenical question, mostly works on the ecumenism of the past thirty years. In spite of this, the reader in search of a history of ecumenism has to refer to Protestant books. There is the extensive English work *History of the Ecumenical Movement*,[10] written under the auspices of the Ecumenical Council of Churches. *Brève Histoire de l'Oecuménisme* (1958) by Pastor Paul Conord might also be read. This brief work, which is easily read and is well organized, deals with Protestant ecumenism, and above all with the Reformed Church of France. It is par-

---

[1] *L'Union des Eglises et le Christianisme*, 1927.

[2] *L'abbé Paul Couturier, apôtre de l'unité chrétienne*, 1957; *Introduction à l'Oecuménisme*, 1958.

[3] *One and Holy*, 1951.

[4] *Le Saint-Siège et l'Union des Eglises*, 1947; *Problemes de l'Unité Chrétienne*, 1950.

[5] *One Shepherd*, 1952.

[6] *Divided Christendom*, 1939; *Vraie et Fausse Reforme dans l'Eglise*, 1950.

[7] *Les Voies de l'Unité Chrétienne*, 1954.

[8] *The Spirit and Forms of Protestantism*, 1956.

[9] *Histoire Doctrinale du Mouvement Oecuménique*, 1955.

[10] Edited by Ruth Rouse and Stephen Neill, 1954.

ticularly useful to the French reader because it indicates the principal lines of development of ecumenical thought among French Protestants. The first work cited, the large *History of the Ecumenical Movement* is an indispensable reference book. However, it explicitly treats the Roman Catholic contribution to the ecumenical dialogue beginning only with 1910. It gives but a fragmentary account up to this date. From this date on it gives a very brief, but objective account. This work doesn't mention the existence of a theology of ecumenism among Catholics, but gives most of its attention to the official aspects of the Catholic attitude towards the ecumenical movement. There are obvious gaps in it.

The present work makes no pretense at filling up these gaps completely. There's still room for a study of ecumenical efforts on the part of Catholics from the time of the Reformation up to the present day. It would also be possible to show what relationships, sometimes astonishingly narrow, existed before the 19th century between the Catholic Church and the Orthodox Churches, despite the official schism that divided them. The interpretation of canonical restrictions concerning "communicatio in sacris" has now become stricter than it ever was before in matters pertaining to Eastern Orthodoxy. It would take a book to write about the progressive separation of the Catholic and Orthodox Churches both before and after the schism. A curve of regression could be traced beginning with a practice which was previously a lot more "ecumenical" than it is in our day. This is not the subject of the present book, however.

In a chapter of *The Catholic Approach to Protestantism* (1955), I briefly indicated some of the historical "bridges" of Catholic ecumenism. The following pages have the sole purpose of taking up this question relative to the genesis and development of modern Catholic ecumenism. Since ecumenism is above all an intellectual movement, I have given special attention to the development of thought. The facts have meaning only by virtue of the concepts which they express. Practical efforts towards reunion achieve their full meaning in the framework of the theology which they represent. Even though I feel that I haven't omitted a single fact worth mentioning, the primary task of this study is to put into focus theological viewpoints in light of their historical development.

It has obviously been necessary to speak about Orthodox and Protestant movements. They are not of principal importance in this work, but we can't speak of Catholic ecumenism without taking into account the ecumenism of the separated Christians whom Catholics meet face to face in interconfessional dialogues. I have endeavored to repeat as little as possible of what I have previously written on this subject. *The Catholic Approach to Protestantism* and *Protestantism* (1959) both deal with recent ecumenical movements. I have been obliged to repeat certain factual information here, and my evaluation remains unchanged on the whole.

The following technical terms will prove useful to the reader:

The words *ecumenism, ecumenist,* and *ecumenical* have taken on a new meaning relative to the unity of separated Christians. The traditional meaning of *ecumenical* is equivalent to *universal.* More recently it refers to the movement of thought and action which is concerned with the reunion of Christians. It is in this latter sense that we generally use it here. The words *ecumenism* and *ecumenist* designate respectively the movement towards the reunion of Christians and the people who are involved.

By *Protestant ecumenism* I understand the ecumenical thought and action which develops in Protestantism. It follows that this expression will also occasionally designate the ecumenical thought which has Protestant unity in view.

Catholic ecumenism includes the ecumenical thought and action developed within Catholicism. It follows that this term can refer to all ecumenical thought which has in mind a unity that would include Catholicism.

The expression *spiritual ecumenism* was coined by Father

Paul Couturier, and refers to a concept of ecumenical effort which gives predominance to piety and spiritual understanding. Father Maurice Villain uses the term *ecumenical technique*. It is applied to the technical knowledge necessary to the apostle of ecumenism. I will not use this term.

The word *Catholic* will not always be used in its proper sense of "Roman Catholic." The word "catholicizing" cannot always be used to designate tendencies, especially Anglican and Lutheran, which approach Catholicism. Whenever the context seems clear enough to avoid equivocation, the word *Catholic* will be used in this sense.

Like my other writings, this is intended primarily for Catholics, who are new to ecumenism, but it doesn't exclude Protestants by any means. The latter will gain a better knowledge of Catholic ecumenism from it. They will gain an appreciation for the efforts made by their Catholic brethren and for the prayers which have been offered up in their search for Christian reunion. I have tried to present Protestantism and ecumenism in a calm light, without thereby giving way to a false irenicism that covers up dogmatic differences and practical difficulties, thus giving an inaccurate idea of what can possibly be realized in the immediate future in the realm of Christian reunion.

May this study inspire fresh enthusiasm for the tremendous task of reuniting Christians in the One Church of Jesus Christ. May it again stir up souls to make the generous sacrifices that that distant day calls for.

—GEORGE H. TAVARD

Mount Mercy College
Pittsburgh, Pennsylvania

CHAPTER I

SCHISMS AND REUNIONS

"We must count among the worst evils of our time the fact that the Churches are separated from one another to the extent that a human society scarcely exists among us, much less that holy communion of the members of Christ, which all profess by their works, but which few sincerely seek in reality."

—John Calvin

However urgent the ecumenical problem has become, it is not new. It has existed since the first schisms among Christians. Those schisms are not of recent origin. Ecumenism, therefore, is not the result of a recent discovery. Though it has not always been known by that name, it is a problem that has been posed by all separations among Christians. Ancient schisms still exist which have yet to be remedied. In the various epochs our fathers have made efforts, crowned with varying degrees of success, to reinstate the severed branches of Christianity into the unity of the one Church. Before taking up the history of ecumenism properly so-called, it is expedient to take the ancient schisms into account, the efforts made to heal them, the success and above all the lack of suc-

13

cess met along the way. All of this constitutes a pre-ecumenism, so to speak, heralding the ecumenism of today.

It is useless for us to waste time on the various heretical factions of the second and third centuries, as they have long since disappeared. The same is true of the Arian heresy, which separated Christians for many centuries, beginning with the fourth. In the fourth and fifth centuries the dreadful Donatist schism cut asunder North African Christendom in the time of Saint Augustine. But neither of these exists today. In the middle ages a schism took place in the very heart of Christian Europe. From 1378 to 1418, two, then three, rival popes fought over the Apostolic See of Rome. The scattered members of western Christendom took sides with one or the other, following the political game of the day. The rivals anathematized and excommunicated each other. The Council of Constance (1414-18) put an end to this scandal. This quarrel, which got everybody so excited, is all but forgotten now. Nevertheless, its importance is indicated by the very name that history has given it: the Great Schism.

On the other hand, there are other schisms, old or relatively new, which still exist. The oldest of these still extant is that of the "Nestorians," who are now on the way to extinction. They derive from the "Nestorian" schism, which followed the Council of Chalcedon (451). They believed in the existence of two natures in Christ but rejected the correlative dogma affirmed by the Church at Chalcedon, namely, the one person of the Word. They appealed to the theology of a patriarch of Constantinople, Nestorius, whence their name. They formed independent Churches in Syria and Mesopotamia. The "Nestorians" were great missionaries; they established churches all over Asia and spread throughout China. The fact that they have totally disappeared from China is one of the mysteries of history. They don't exist today except for small communities in Iraq, and in the United States.

The "Monophysite" Churches, which accept the one person but reject the two natures of Christ, separated themselves from the main Church after the Council of Chalcedon. These Churches still flourish in Armenia, Georgia, Egypt, Ethiopia, the Levant, and on the Malabar coast of India.

The most distressing schism is that which has opposed the four Eastern patriarchs of Constantinople, Alexandria, Antioch and Jerusalem to the Western patriarch of Rome since 1054. In the eyes of the Eastern patriarchs of this period, the pope of Rome was simply *primus inter pares*. In the eyes of the pope of Rome, and in the light of the growing precisions of Eastern theology and canonical practice, the patriarchs of the East were subordinate to that of Rome. This flagrant schism, in which accusations of heresy were interchanged, was the unhappy fruit of a long and painful rivalry between the bishop of Rome and the bishop of Byzantium on the one hand, and between the Frankish kings and the Byzantine Empire on the other. Political claims and religious interests were inextricably confused in the midst of these disputes. The result has been the most tenacious schism Christianity has ever known between bishops sharing the same Christological and sacramental doctrine.

Then in the sixteenth century the West was split by the Protestant Reformation. All of Northern Europe and important sections of Central Europe separated from the Roman communion, not just in matters of discipline but also in matters of faith. Anglicanism and Protestantism, with its two great branches of Lutheranism and Calvinism, became rivals of Catholic Christianity, and claimed to teach the pure doctrine of the Gospel which the bishop of Rome had contaminated in the course of time. Because of its emigration to America and its missionary zeal, Protestantism has since become a world-wide phenomenon.

For the sake of memory, we should also mention a schism which did not involve the Catholic Church, but which affected Russian Orthodox Christianity in the seventeenth century. Liturgical and canonical reforms stirred up the opposition of a large minority in the Russian Orthodox Church. In 1666 it resulted in the "raskol" or schism of the Old Believers or "Starovites." The number of Old Believers was increased when, on January 25, 1721, Tzar Peter the Great suppressed the patriarchate of Moscow, replaced it by the Holy Synod, and imposed vast ecclesiastical reforms. They themselves split into two groups, the *Popovtzi* and the *Bezpopovtzi,* the latter doing away with the priesthood. The Old Believers became very numerous, always maintaining very narrow relations with the official Church. It is impossible to evaluate the condition of the Old Believers since the Bolshevik Revolution.

In the same epoch, the Church of Rome suffered a new schism. The archbishop of Utrecht rejected the condemnation of Jansenism by the Bull *Unigenitus* in 1713, and drew some Dutch Catholics into schism. Later on, this Jansenist Church drew recruits from among the German and Swiss Catholics who rejected the dogma of papal infallibility after the Vatican Council in 1871. It wasn't the first time that a definition of faith provoked a schism. It happened as early as 451 at the close of the Council of Chalcedon. Later, when the dogma of the Assumption was defined, it seemed evident that definitions increase the obstacles to the already difficult task of ecumenical rapprochement, even if they are not the occasion of a schism.

Schisms have also taken place very recently, moreover. The Independent Philippine Church, called the "Aglipayan" Church, separated from Rome at the beginning of this century. After letting Roman episcopal succession lapse, they obtained an episcopacy from the Anglicans. The Polish National Church is made up of American descendants of Polish Catholics who left Catholic unity in 1904 after their arrival in the United States.

The history of the Church is not just a series of schisms. There is also a history of efforts made to regain unity of faith and unity of hearts. Since we can't recount all the events here, we must content ourselves with indicating the most important bridges and mentioning the principal unions that have been effected.

The only reunion of "Nestorians" worth mentioning took place in the sixteenth century when a small fraction joined Rome. The rest continued their independent existence, and have become very weak in the face of Islam's missionary force.

Numerous attempts at union among the Monophysite Churches have met with some degree of success. The Maronite Church, which returned to Catholic communion in 1181, is a former schismatic group that followed Monophysitism. It is concentrated in Syria and Lebanon. A reunion with the Armenians of Cilicia lasted from 1198 to 1375. The Council of Florence (1438-39) attempted a short-lived union of all the Monophysite Churches. The attempts were renewed in the sixteenth century and since then a Syrian Church in union with Rome exists. Negotiations with the Ethiopian Copts in 1628 failed. Agreement was reached with some Egyptian Copts in the seventeenth century. Some of the Armenians united with Rome in the eighteenth century. In the nineteenth century a group of Ethiopian Copts did the same. Finally, in 1930, the reconciliation of a strong minority of Indian Jacobites introduced the Syro-Malankar Rite into the Church.

From the ecumenical point of view these partial reunions, important as they may be, are still tragedies, because they haven't been able to realize union except at the price of a new schism. The Churches thus reunited with the Catholic Communion remain separated from their sister-Churches. The problem of unity as a whole remains a problem with them.

The same remark must be made regarding the constitution of the Churches which are improperly styled "Uniates." They consist of sections of the Orthodox Churches which have rejoined the Roman Communion at some time or other. The

Councils of Lyons in 1274 and of Florence in 1438-39 made a good try at a wholesale reconciliation between Rome and the East. Officially, if not in heart, this union was sealed on two occasions. It was ruptured anew a few years later. Since the fifteenth century only partial reunions have been effected, and they are themselves the source of new tensions with Eastern Orthodoxy. Among the oriental rites united with Rome are the Ruthenian Church since 1595, a Serbian Church, concentrated in the Diocese of Kreutz, since the seventeenth century, a Roumanian Church in union since 1697, the Melkite Church in the Levant since 1701, a small Bulgarian Church since the nineteenth century, and a small group of Greeks since the beginning of the twentieth century.

All official efforts towards reunion have been made on the part of Churches which have faithfully kept the apostolic succession of bishops. The Protestant world has remained apart from these attempts at rapprochement. The Anglican Communion was the object of special interest on the part of the Catholic Church for a short time in the seventeenth century, but this came to nothing.

As a matter of fact, circumstances have caused the problem of rapprochement between Catholics and Anglicans or Protestants to be left up to individual initiative. The violent clashes between Catholics and Reformers had been too frequent and too prolonged for ecumenical enterprises to see a quick turn in their favor. Nevertheless both Catholics and Protestants regretted the lack of unanimity between believers. They prayed for the triumph of truth. Calvin came out with the anguished cry that "one must not abandon the ministers of Christ with any other feeling than of our bowels being torn away from us. . . . One of the worst evils of our time is the fact that there are so many different Churches." [1]

A rapprochement certainly had to be effected between Catholics and Protestants sooner or later, even if only in

---

[1] Quoted by Paul Conord in *Brève Histoire de l'Oecuménisme,* p. 44.

private and on a small scale. A number of theologians were already working at it during the seventeenth and eighteenth centuries.[2] But one can hardly speak of a true movement in this direction before the nineteenth century, so we will fix the birth of contemporary ecumenism in the nineteenth century.

---

[2] See *The Catholic Approach to Protestantism*, ch. 9.

PART **one**

THE

NINETEENTH

CENTURY

CHAPTER **II**

BEGINNINGS

> *"The idea of the true Church here given is not realized in one single instance, but by the peaceful cosmopolitan union of all existing communions, each being as perfect as possible after its own manner."*
>
> —Friedrich Schleiermacher

The ecumenical movement properly speaking did not see the light of day in Protestantism until towards the end of the nineteenth century. It could not be born, however, without an incubation period. Nothing of consequence takes place without preparation. It is always hard for precursors to give an account of the direction they are unconsciously following. But it is always relatively easy for latecomers to analyze after the event the tendencies which have blossomed into great things. As a matter of fact, the Protestantism of the first half of the nineteenth century served as a stage on which multiple factors of union were at play. Their convergence made later ecumenical projects possible.

On the whole, the centrifugal force which multiplied the confessions of faith born of the Reformation was practically spent by the end of the eighteenth century. Calvinism and

23

Lutheranism came under influences which brought them closer together from the doctrinal point of view. The differences which distinguished the Calvinist Reformation from the Lutheran Reformation did not pertain essentially to the faith. Calvinism and Lutheranism were in agreement as far as the principal foundations of the sixteenth century Reformation were concerned. They both held Scripture to be the sole rule of faith, and the correlative principle of justification by grace alone. The differences arose when it came to defining with some accuracy certain practices of faith, particularly the Last Supper. Here theological explanations varied. In the course of the eighteenth century, however, Lutheranism and Calvinism sustained somewhat equalizing influences. In Germany, as in England and France, Protestantism took a rather novel mystic turn. This mysticism caused schisms, especially in England, where it could not flourish in the organized Churches, but had a tendency to unite the Churches that welcomed it, through a return to the Gospel sources.

Thus German pietism, which was a decided characteristic of the Lutheran Churches, was only a manifestation of a very widespread evangelical renewal. This renewal gave rise to Methodism in England. It penetrated American Calvinism through the Great Revivals of 1740 and 1800. It stirred up French Calvinism during the Revival of 1830.

But if doctrine sometimes divides, love and piety unite. Thus it is not purely by accident that one of the great precursors of Protestant ecumenism was Count Zinzendorf (1700-60), a tireless advocate of pietism. He felt that all Christianity, Catholicism included, could be united through the influence of pietist communities scattered throughout all the Churches. Before him, the Englishman John Dury (1596-1680) had been affected by nascent pietism. In America, during the second half of the eighteenth century, the preachers of the Great Revival became all things to all men. Using, as it were, all wood for fuel, they preached from the pulpits of every Church, whether Baptist, Congregationalist, Presby-

terian or Methodist. Throughout that entire century, moreover, the itinerant preachers who took care of the religious
needs of the American pioneers paid little attention to confessional differences. Thus they prepared Protestantism in the
United States for the great ecumenical tasks. Pietist renovation also left its mark on Anglicanism in the form of what is
called evangelism. It put new life into the most Protestant
elements of the Church of England.

By means of a common piety and a common spirit in the
Lord, in the living joy of His gifts, all these movements, even
if they sometimes seem to have no connection with each
other, provided Protestantism on the whole with a vision of
Christian unity. This vision eventually inspired definite projects.

The hour struck in the second half of the nineteenth century. In 1847 the *Universal Evangelical Alliance,* largely
motivated by revival pietism, was born. But the Alliance was
an inter-confessional society. It seems in fact that it was the
first to use the word "ecumenism" in the modern sense of
the word, credit for which is due to the Frenchman Adolphe
Monod.[1] Societies of Christian youth were established along
the same line. The *Young Men's Christian Association*
(YMCA), founded in 1878, and its counterpart the *Young
Women's Christian Association,* 1894, had their origin in
inter-confessional pietist movements. These were federations
of local inter-confessional societies, the oldest of which was
founded in London in 1844. The *World Federation of Christian Students,* established in 1895 by the American John
Mott (1865-1955), perpetuated this inter-confessional tradition.

The nineteenth century was also a time for reshuffling.
Churches having identical origin but which were separated
geographically became interested in one another more than
ever before. They attempted to preserve unbroken relations.

---

[1] See Paul Conord, *op. cit.,* p. 206.

Thus the *Reformed Churches' Alliance* was established in 1875. In 1881 twenty-eight Churches were represented at a world-wide Methodist conference. An *International Congregationalist Council* met for the first time in 1891. After extensive preparations, the Baptist Churches held a similar reunion in 1905.

In one way or other, all this fermentation of the idea of unity derived from the pietist and evangelical renewal. In the eyes of the historian it is symptomatic of a progressive unification of Protestantism. Before trying to reunite Churches professing opposite doctrines, it is necessary to reconcile those having the same origin and the same theology. In large measure this was the work of the second half of the nineteenth century.

There was another Protestant current developing at this time. The liberal element must not be omitted from a study of the sources of Protestant ecumenism, because, on the whole, liberalism was also the common experience of Protestantism. It was likewise a leveling factor despite variations in origin and different heritages.

Protestant liberalism might be represented as a religious transformation of the philosophical rationalism that was popular in the eighteenth century. Rationalism submitted religion to the norms of natural reason, without reference to any supernatural revelation. It wanted to absorb every cult, Christianity included, into a purely natural religion. Protestant liberalism does not go that far. On the contrary, it wants to be religious, and in a sense, supernatural. It places Christ and His revelation in the center of religious history. But it does not see the relevance of dogma. In attempting to make Christianity respectable in the eyes of rationalist philosophy, it ends up with a reinterpretation of the faith. Rationalism believes it can destroy revealed religion by showing the absurdity of dogmas. As a result, liberal Protestantism, that of Friedrich Schleiermacher (1768-1834) among others, does not deny the absurdity of dogmas if they are taken literally.

It doesn't deny the efficacy of the rationalist critique. It only aims at reestablishing the value of religion on a level that avoids this criticism. For that purpose an area must be found that is beyond the reach of analytical reasoning. Schleiermacher found it in experience. Thus religion consists in being "one with the Eternal in the unity of intuition and feeling which is immediate." [2] Dogmas are sublimated. Their formulas remain the same, but their substance changes. Schleiermacher asks himself: "What is the operation of grace?" And he answers: "Nothing else, manifestly, than the common expression for interchange between the entrance of the world into man through intuition and feeling, and the outgoing of man into the world through action and culture." [3]

Religious liberalism tends by nature to give all religions one common denominator, the experience of the mysterious depths of existence through which man divines or perceives God obscurely. Thus liberalism has favored the inclusion of divergent traditions in a common basic experience. This stage in the Protestant evolution could not help but harm the doctrinal substance of Protestantism. Protestant liberalism undoubtedly was better off than philosophical rationalism, but it let itself be dragged along by it onto the shifting sands of relativism. In its attempt to answer the latter's questions and to escape its negative criticism, it made the mistake of situating the essence of Christianity in immediate intuition and religious feeling. What happens then to historic revelation, to the figure of Christ taught by tradition? The faith is no longer the believing faith of the Scholastics nor the trusting faith of the Reformers. It becomes a perception of the religious "sub-soil" of the human conscience and an obedience to the religious tendencies innate in man.

Liberal Protestantism developed during the nineteenth century. One might say, at the cost of making a generalization, that it changed from the primacy of religious conscience, in

---

[2] *On Religion*, Harper Torchbooks, 1959, p. 40.
[3] *Ibid.*, p. 901.

Schleiermacher's sense, to the primacy of moral conscience. Religious conscience or "feeling" was again a product of pietism. Pietism became unfashionable in the positivist and scientific atmosphere of the nineteenth century. One had to attach the very enfeebled Christianity of liberal Protestantism to something more tangible than religious conscience. One had recourse to moral conscience. The Frenchman Charles Secretan was then able to write: "The miracle of the Incarnation of the Son is none other than the moral fact of conversion taken as the center of history and of humanity." [4]

With the widespread development of the social problem in the second half of the century, this moral Christianity becomes a "social Christianity" preaching the "social gospel." Christianity was no longer a faith, either in the Catholic sense or in the Lutheran sense of the word. It became a service to the community, and Christ was the highest model to emulate, not the Son of God made man.

Liberal Protestantism orientated the Churches toward a new view of their mutual relationships. Doctrinal differences disappeared, giving way to a universal religious conscience, to a moral ideal common to humanity, or to a study of social disorders. Just like evangelism, liberalism brought forward a new statement of the problem of Christian unity.

The nineteenth century witnessed the Protestant Churches being invaded by the so-called historical method. Liberal Protestantism, sensitive to contemporary cultural currents, subscribed to the scientific historical school of thought. History set the tone for everything. But historicism easily confused history with the historian. The historian became the high priest of a new kind of Christianity. He was expected to decide what was still tenable in traditional faith, and what historical science, in its infallibility, had shown to be false. As a consequence, the historical method prepared a climate that made the ecumenical problem intelligible.

---

[4] Quoted by Jacques de Senarclens in *Héretiers de la Reformation,* 1956, p. 84-5.

Despite its methods, which were questionable because they were over-ambitious and not sufficiently given to self-criticism, the study of the historical Jesus replaced the Bible, as a document, at the focus of Protestant concerns. Unconsciously this counterbalanced the trends that concentrated their attention on the religious conscience or the moral conscience. It then inspired a secondary effect: a return to the Bible sources. Theories regarding the historical value of the Scriptures and the historical personality of Jesus were sometimes capable of going too far. Christianity, seen in the light of the comparative history of religions, could lose its absolute value and devolve into a history of one redemption among others. For August Sabatier, in his *Outline of a Philosophy of Religion based on Psychology and History* (1901), the essence of Christianity is a "sense of history" manifesting "the vital process which is created by the infinite and eternal Spirit." [5] Any kind of religion may fit this description. It nevertheless remains true that historical research favors a daily contact with the text of Scripture itself, thus encouraging a fresh reading of the Bible.

The Bible was no longer studied mainly through the confessional books of Protestantism or the commentaries of the Reformers. One unforeseen consequence of this sometimes puerile enthusiasm for the historical method in the study of Christian sources was to bring back to the text of the Scriptures themselves a Protestantism that was already pretty far removed from the Reformers' writings. By that very fact Protestant theology found itself ushered onto the path of Scripture and it was able to hear the echo of the word of God.

Protestant missionary expansion attained vast proportions in the course of the nineteenth century. To a great extent the missionary movement was inspired by pietism. Evangelical zeal led the Protestant missionaries to the far corners of Africa and Asia. They preached the Gospel of Jesus Christ

---

[5] Quoted by Jacques de Senarclens, *op. cit.,* p. 100.

such as they knew it. Influenced by evangelism, they attached little importance to confessional differences. Being isolated among pagan peoples, they were glad to collaborate and to help each other out whenever the occasion demanded, regardless of whatever Church they might happen to belong to. Being men of good sense, they did not like to preach against the other Churches. They felt how incongruous it would be to import sixteenth century European religious quarrels into India or Madagascar.

The missionary societies which financed evangelization looked favorably on this sort of inter-confessionalism. Up until 1814 the Anglican "Society For the Promotion of Christian Knowledge" (SPCK), which was founded in 1699, had sent only Lutheran ministers to India. As a point of fact, missionaries organized the first conferences that may be called ecumenical. Though proposed as early as 1806, these meetings did not take place until 1854. But once one of them had been held, there was no difficulty organizing others. The missionary societies were represented at these conferences in large numbers.

To summarize it all, nineteenth century Protestantism clearly put the Churches on the way towards progressive unification. This evolution was the work of the pioneers who started inter-confessional gatherings, sometimes at the cost of great efforts. It was also the dream of generous-hearted visionaries who proposed plans for union, all of which were more or less utopian. Above all, it was the fruit of a profound theological undertow that moved the Churches and that brought them together, oftentimes without their being aware of the fact.

CHAPTER III

PROPHETIC VOICES

*"Aren't Catholicism and Protestantism related to each
other like a building which cannot stand, to a buttress
which cannot stand alone, whereas the whole is even
very firm and secure, so long as they keep together, the
building and the buttress which supports it?"*

—Kierkegaard

The nineteenth century wasn't a choice period for liberal
Protestantism alone. No doubt dogmas lost their importance
in large sections of the Lutheran and Calvinist Churches.
Nevertheless, symptoms of a reaction appeared. This confessional renewal was due to spread in the twentieth century
and affect Anglicanism and Lutheranism in particular. It has
necessarily had indirect consequences in the contemporary
ecumenical movement. Otherwise the Protestant equalizing
tendency that dominated the nineteenth century could have
resulted in a Pan-Protestantism. The desire for Christian
unity would have resolved itself into a simple desire for Protestant unity.

In 1806 French Protestantism had already raised the question of a union of all Christians belonging to the Reformation Churches. Pierre Antoine Rabaut, called Rabaut the Younger (1765-1808), was following a longstanding tradition of French Protestantism. Despite the persecutions that it sustained, first during the religious wars (1562-95), then as a consequence of the revocation of the Edict of Nantes (1685),[1] French Protestantism never turned sectarian. It knew how to preserve a generosity of spirit and a universal consciousness that has oftentimes been lacking in Protestants of other countries. However, Rabaut the Young's work entitled *Historical Details and Collection of Documents on the Projects of Reunion Which Have Been Conceived up to the Present Day for the Reunion of all the Reformation Churches,* had only Protestant reunion in mind, and did not consider the problem of Catholicism. But it ought to be evident, even to the most conservative Protestants, that no reunion could possibly result in a Christian unity that would close the door to the Catholic Church and the Orthodox Churches. Precisely, the Catholicizing renewal of Lutheranism and Anglicanism during the nineteenth century allowed the desire for union to avoid a certain narrowness which would have condemned it to failure right from the very start.

The reawakening of Lutheran confessionalism in Germany might be dated from the third centenary of Martin Luther's fixing his ninety-five theses on the door of the castle church of Wittenberg.

To commemorate this event, Klaus Harms (1778-1855) published ninety-five theses in 1817 in which he reacted against the theology of the Enlightenment, and against the Calvinist-Lutheran union which had been imposed on the Prussian Churches by King Frederic Wilhelm III. It was at the time that Schleiermacher wrote a system of dogmatics (Glaubenslehre, 1821) which, in an air of utter religiosity,

---

[1] Regarding the spread of persecutions of French Protestants in the 16th century, see Samuel Mours' *Le Protestantisme en France au XVIe siècle,* Paris, 1959.

proposed a symbolic explanation of dogmas. Klaus Harms, on the other hand, outlined a return to Luther's confessionalism. Thus, Lutheranism was urged to reclaim itself and never to give itself up again to a vague Christianity lacking a traditional theological framework. This renewal of Lutheran confessionalism bore fruit in 1833 when Adolf Harless (1806-79) began teaching at the University of Erlangen. What has been referred to as the school of Erlangen insisted, following Harless, on the objective reality of the Christological doctrines, of the sacraments, and of the Church, as being the very foundation of Lutheran Protestantism. Without being isolated from German philosophy, the theologians of Erlangen and their followers at the University of Leipzig brought theology back to the Lutheran confessional books as well as to Scripture. The names of Johan Hofmann (1810-77) and Gottfried Thomasius (1802-75) might be mentioned in connection with Harless. The "High Church" (hoch-Kirche) movement which shows up in the modern Lutheran liturgical revival is a result of this confessional reaction of the past century. This ensured that the desire for union which has grown since the beginning of the nineteenth century would respect doctrine and would not be realized at the cost of abandoning dogmas.

Lutheranism's contribution to nascent ecumenism did not consist solely in protecting concern for doctrine. A concern such as this is clearly a positive one, because insistence on dogma is certainly not negative. It means calling us back to the Revelation. Lutheranism has in fact gone quite far in this direction. With the Dane Nicolai Grundtvig (1783-1872) it elaborated a theology that is truly universal in its scope.

A theologian, historian, poet, and specialist in Scandinavian mythology, Grundtvig did not deal expressly with the ecumenical problem. His name is not even mentioned in the index of Rouse and Neill's *History of the Ecumenical Movement*. This is a surprising omission. Those men who are explicitly preoccupied with union are not the only ones who

are to be counted among the precursors of ecumenism. It is
also fitting to recognize those who have proposed a theology
of unity.

Grundtvig deserves mention in this second category. In the
midst of what appeared to him as the rationalist decadence
of Danish Lutheranism, Grundtvig inaugurated a confessional
return to primitive Lutheranism. Thus he belongs among the
builders of modern Lutheranism, like the German theologians
that we have mentioned. Grundtvig reached beyond Lutheranism on more than one point, however. For him, Scripture
was not the foundation of faith. Scripture itself comes from
the Church and therefore should not be taken as its foundation. "I have discovered a truth," he avowed, "we do not
find the Church in Scripture, but Scripture in the Church." [2]

Furthermore, Scripture would be a dead letter without the
Spirit which breathes in the Church. Then what is the Church?
According to Grundtvig, the Church is no denomination in
particular. Among the denominations, Grundtvig, momentarily puzzled by Catholicism, condemned the Church of
Rome more and more vehemently. If he initiated a return to
the sacraments and to doctrine, Grundtvig never encouraged
a rapprochement with Roman Catholicism. But if he anathematized the "pope," that is to say, any hierarchic system of
government, he no less vigorously opposed the "anti-pope,"
i.e., any ecclesiastical system founded on the infallibility of
a book, even the Bible. The Church, in Grundtvig's mind, is
not a system. It is a brotherly community born of the Spirit
in an intercommunion of God and man. The intercommunion
which constitutes the Church, according to the "discovery"
Grundtvig made shortly after 1825, is Baptism. The infallible
doctrine professed by the Church is no other than the *credo,*
which is affirmed in the course of every Baptism since the
earliest days of Christianity. It is not a written, but a recited
credo, in which the voice of the Spirit Himself is heard. This

---

[2] Quoted by Renest S. Nielsen in *N.F.S. Grundtvig,* 1955, p. 78.

credo, affirmed through all ages and by all Churches, constitutes the fundamental unity of the Church.

In the name of this unity, Grundtvig doesn't hesitate to denounce a "teacher of lies." He would make such a pronouncement "in the name of the Church which was, which is, and which shall be, and whose doctrine is clearly manifested in its history, in the name of the one, true, historic Christian Church." [3] One sole Christian unanimity exists from which no one can separate himself without apostatizing. "It is undeniable," said Grundtvig, "that those who believe and who hope what all Christians confess are the only true Christians." [4] The unanimity of the *credo* manifests itself sacramentally. Not just Baptism, but the Eucharist too is a sacrament of the unanimity of the faith. Grundtvig eloquently described this sacramental and doctrinal unity of the Church: "I see the Redeemer reflected in the congregation, both old and new, celebrating the Lord's Supper, partaking of the bread and the chalice and exclaiming in an outburst of love: 'Numerous as we are, we are one bread, one body, just as we have also received the same Spirit and were vivified by the same hope.' Yes, one Saviour, one Faith, one Baptism, one God, the Father of all, who is above all, among all, and in all." [5]

Let the Churches and denominations be. According to Grundtvig they are simply "schools." They have constructed different theologies, even opposing systems. They achieve their worth not from their theologies and their systems but through their respect for the one Church, born of Baptism and manifesting itself in the *credo* of universal tradition.

Grundtvig certainly could not be called the father of Protestant ecumenism. His work nevertheless involves a theology of Christian unity which provides numerous points of contact

---

[3] Quoted by Hal Koch in *Grundtvig* (English trans.), 1952, p. 91.
[4] Nielsen, *ibid.,* p. 80.
[5] Nielsen, *ibid.,* p. 23.

with current thought. It is surprising that the official ecumenical movement doesn't take better advantage of it.

Another great name in the Danish Church of this epoch is Søren Kierkegaard (1813-55). The father of the existential dialectic was not directly concerned with the problems of Christian unity. His thought has nonetheless influenced the doctrinal renewal of modern Protestantism. Kierkegaard has been slowly recognized as one of the great philosophers of our time. From the theological point of view, he has been neglected even longer.

However, the religious critique of Danish liberal Protestantism has made Kierkegaard a precursor of the return to the Gospel that is playing a significant role in the development of the ecumenical movement. Kierkegaard clearly affirmed the relativity of Protestantism. "Protestantism, Christianly considered, is quite simply an untruth, a piece of dishonesty which falsifies the teaching, the world-view, the life-view of Christianity, just as soon as it is regarded as a principle for Christianity, not as a remedy at a given time and place." [6] Here we have one of those statements that spells the ruin of any eternalization of Protestantism. An attempt to achieve a purely Protestant union would deny as a matter of principle that Catholicism is part of Christianity. But we know from Kierkegaard's journal that he willingly looked up to the Catholic Church.

On the one hand, Kierkegaard affirmed the ultimate defeat of the Reformation: "Lutheranism is a corrective, but a corrective made into the norm, the whole, is *eo ipso* confusing in the next generation, when that which it was meant to correct no longer exists." [7] On the other hand, in calling Protestantism back to the Christianity of the Gospel, Kierkegaard directed his readers towards certain values which were

---

[6] *Attack on Christendom,* trans., by Walter Lowrie, Beacon Press edition, 1944, p. 34.

[7] *Journal (1854),* ed. by Alexander Dru, Harper Torchbooks, 1959, p. 232.

lost by Protestants, but always kept alive in Catholicism. The monastic ideal, among other things, seemed to him to be an echo of primitive asceticism which the bourgeois Protestantism of his day was lacking. Thus Kierkegaard dared to write: "Christianity's first and foremost duty is to return to the monastery from which Luther broke away." [8] The Danish prophet thereby merits being counted among the builders of the Catholic renewal in Lutheranism, and more indirectly, in Protestantism as a whole.

As for the rest, all of Kierkegaard's religious thought affirms one thing: the official Christianity of the Churches no longer has any justification if it does not correspond to the fundamental Christianity of the soul abandoned to God in faith, and to what he called, in the title of a volume of his *Edifying Discourses,* the "works of love." But this love is manifested in Catholicism as well as in Protestantism. No unity is Christian that doesn't strive to gather all lovers of Christ into a whole.

No doubt Kierkegaard, suspicious of large numbers as he was, was hardly anxious to preach a reunion of that kind. Rather, his true Christians appeared as isolated individuals in the midst of the official apostate Churches, whose works did not conform to their words, and whose words themselves no longer reflected those of Christ. Perhaps we may find here an incipient spiritual ecumenism which would enlist individuals, but not Churches. It would be far removed from the concern of a Christian organism that is in the heart of Catholicism and of the Catholicizing currents of Anglicanism and Protestantism.

Therefore Kierkegaard's contribution to ecumenical thought remains equivocal. Still, Kierkegaard permitted a new look at Catholicism. He must be considered, at least because of his posthumous influence, as one of the thinkers who have introduced Protestantism to the agonizing burden

---

[8] *Ibid.,* p. 240.

of unity. His return to the Gospel sources, bypassing the structures of official Protestantism, made it easier to take up the question of Catholic unity without insurmountable prejudice.

Lutheranism wasn't satisfied, then, with making a step towards Protestant brotherhood. With the Schools of Erlangen and Leipzig it openly returned to the Orthodoxy that had dominated the seventeenth century. This didn't come about without hesitation. The biggest names in German theology continued in the path of liberalism. They even took the first places in world-wide liberal Protestantism without great difficulty. After Schleiermacher, the master of many Protestant generations, Albrecht Ritschl (1822-89) and Adolf Harnack (1851-1930) dominated the Protestant world. A trend that was at first in the minority nevertheless increased. It would eventually result in today's "High Church" renewal. Perhaps in spite of itself, as was the case with Grundtvig, it directed Lutheranism somewhat timorously towards the question of Catholic unity. Søren Kierkegaard's critique of liberalism was destined to give greater assurance and forcefulness to this movement.

The question of Catholic unity as such had not yet been explicitly proposed. It was the task of Anglicanism to introduce this discussion.

CHAPTER IV

OXFORD

> *"If the sixteenth century was one of dispersion, the nine-*
> *teenth and twentieth must be one of reunion, if the Son*
> *of Man, when He cometh, is to find the faith on the*
> *earth."*
> —Alexander Forbes

The Catholic renewal of Lutheranism did not extend so far
as the analogous movement which shook Anglicanism in the
nineteenth century. A long tradition in the Church of England brought it closer to the Catholic Church. From the out-
set the English Reformation had taken a route different from
that of Protestantism pure and simple. Apart from a genuinely
Protestant stream which formed several branches as time
went on, there were always some Catholic tendencies alive.
These dominated Anglicanism during the first two-thirds of
the seventeenth century. The Revolution of 1688 and the
exile of King James II reduced them to a defensive position.
During the eighteenth century the more Catholic tendencies
in the Church of England, isolated during the Non-Jurors'
schism, all but disappeared from Anglicanism. They were

hardly represented at the beginning of the nineteenth century except by small groups leading a rear-guard action for the defense of Catholic principles. Most schools of thought leaned increasingly towards continental Protestantism. With the Evangelical movement, Anglicanism knew an original form of pietism nourished by the *Book of Common Prayer*. Under the sway of rationalism, some of its members looked on the Anglican Church as the most reasonable form of Christianity. With the triumph of liberal Protestantism, they underwent the universal craze for scientism, biblicism, and historicism.

The decay of the "High Church" tradition was stemmed by the Oxford Movement. In the work of John Keble (1792-1866), Edward Pusey (1800-82) and John Henry Newman (1801-90), the "Tractarians" restored a Catholic interpretation of Anglicanism almost at a single stroke. This effort led Newman into the Catholic Church. But the Catholic interpretation of the Thirty-Nine Articles set forth in his Tract 90 remained the charter of Anglo-Catholicism.

After Newman's departure the Oxford Movement undertook a vast liturgical reform that went more and more in the direction of the Roman liturgy. But the essential contribution of the movement lay with its doctrinal restorations. Like the Caroline divines of the seventeenth century, the Tractarians saw the Anglican Church as the Catholic Church herself, in full continuity with the Church of the Middle Ages and the Church of the Fathers. They insisted on the non-Protestantism of the Anglican tradition in its better aspects more than the Caroline divines did. They also surpassed them in affirming certain Catholic doctrines which henceforth they knew not to be "Papist" injunctions but the authentic doctrine of the Fathers of the Church.

The ecumenical interest of the Oxford movement isn't immediately apparent, however, if it is judged from a Lutheran or Calvinist point of view. The consequences of a Catholic revival in Anglicanism are nevertheless vast as far as the problem of Christian unity is concerned.

The fact that a growing section of Anglicans looked on the Protestant Reformation with suspicion made it impossible to establish an ecumenism based solely on the foundations of the sixteenth century Reformation. Thanks to the Oxford Movement, any desire for Christian reunion had to aspire to something more than a pietist type of unity or a confessional unity founded on Reformist formulas of faith. The Christian youth societies, influenced by pietism, became old-fashioned before they were even born. The dream of a world-wide missionary Protestantism having a simply practical purpose became unwillingly utopian. Ever since the start of the Oxford Movement, no Christian reunion can succeed, even one designed by Protestants, unless it is solidly founded on the doctrine of the Fathers of the Church. This holds true even outside the Catholic and Orthodox worlds. The guides and leaders of the Protestant ecumenical movement have not readily accepted this as a fact. Perhaps they still hope that things will change. This does not excuse them from the obligation to face facts. Every dream of a Pan-Protestant union has to exclude the Anglican communion, unless, which God forbid, the Anglican communion be willing to pay for such a union with a renunciation of the soundest theological element of its rightful tradition.

The return of Anglicanism to a patristic theology and its restoration of a Catholic liturgy was bound to raise the question of union with the Orthodox Churches, faithful holders of the Greek patristic tradition, and with the Catholic Church. This question was undoubtedly not at first raised with a view to universal Christian reunion. In a just reversal of positions, the heirs of the theology of the Non-Jurors, who had been expelled from the Established Church, had gladly considered a Christian unity that would leave Protestants out of the picture. In fact, Newman and his friends elaborated a theology of the Church which was at the same time a theology of unity. The unity they described in the famous "branch theory" clearly excluded Protestantism. The Church was one, but, in the image of the Holy Trinity, one in three. Eastern Orthodoxy, Roman Catholicism, and Anglo-Catholicism formed the three branches, of different origin but of equal value, of the one Church. As for the fundamental marks of the Church, as Newman explains in his *Apologia pro Vita Sua,* Rome seems to have emphasized Apostolicity, while Anglicanism has flourished through its Catholicity. Their destiny was to unite in the eyes of men as they were already one in the eyes of God. Newman prayed for the unity of the universal Church: "I wished for union between the Anglican Church and Rome if and when it was possible; and I did what I could to gain weekly prayers for that object." [1]

Since he saw Anglicanism as a "branch" of the Catholic Church, Newman condemned Lutheranism and Calvinism as "heresies, repugnant to Scripture, springing up three centuries since, and anathematized by East as well as West." [2]

The only Christian unity in the eyes of the Oxford Movement then, is Catholic unity. This excluded, a priori, Protestantism. It can only be a question of uniting the Roman Catholic Church, the Orthodox Church, and the Anglican Church, after having purified the latter of its most Protestant elements.

This was evidently insufficient as a formula of ecumenism. Unless the ecumenical movement disregarded an important part of Christianity, it could not start off on such a basis. Otherwise it would have been conceivable, if at least the question had been raised, that two ecumenical movements could appear. One, within Protestantism, would work for the union of Lutherans, Calvinists, the English Free Churches, and the Protestants of the New World. A parallel but opposed movement, on the other hand, would concern itself with the question of Catholic reunion on the part of the three "branches" of the Church.

---

[1] *Apologia pro Vita Sua,* Doubleday, New York, 1956, p. 225.
[2] *Ibid.,* p. 243.

Fortunately, things didn't turn out that way. Forces were to appear later which united the Protestant and the Catholic concerns for unity. Despite the widely separated positions of the Oxford Movement and the present-day ideas of the ecumenical movement, there is one thing that should be recognized. The "Tractarians" performed a truly prophetic work when they brought up the problem of Christian unity neither on the rather pietistic plane of a union of hearts, nor even on the level of doctrinal unity, which could be a Lutheran or a Catholic concern, but on that of a union of Churches. They visualized reunion only as a group phenomenon, as a collective rapprochement of one body with another, as a reaching out of one Church toward another, of a tradition toward a tradition. Newman himself gave the example for individual conversion, yet he was disturbed over the consequences such conversions have on the reunion of Churches. "I think," he wrote in 1857, "that it is for the interest of Catholicism that individuals should not join us, but should remain to leaven the mass. I mean that they will do more for us by remaining where they are than by coming over." [3] It is true that Newman questioned himself at the same time as to just what these people would become. "But then they have individual souls, and with what heart can I do anything to induce them to preach to others, if they themselves thereby become castaways?" Whatever be the demands of the individual conscience leading to conversion, the true problem of unity is on the collective level.

After 1850, in an attempt to resolve the problem of collective rapprochements, the Oxford Movement considered a solution: corporate reunion. The builders of the Oxford Movement were not too enthusiastic about corporate reunion, but they couldn't ignore the fact that corporate reunion was Pusey's constant ideal, as it was for Newman before his conversion. Some excited individuals have not per-

[3] Letter to Phillips de Lisle. See E. C. Purcell, *Life and Letters of Ambrose Phillips de Lisle,* London, Macmillan, 1900, v. I, p. 368.

ceived the harm that unreasonable zeal for individual conversions has done to collective rapprochements. Any objective observer must be aware of the fact that each departure of an Anglo-Catholic weakens Anglo-Catholicism, which thereby becomes suspect to those with other Anglican theological tendencies. It adds to the difficulty of Anglicanism's return as a body to the most Catholic elements in its tradition. It brings Anglicanism closer to Protestantism and to that extent further from Catholicism. To verify these facts is only a matter of observation. It cannot, in all justice, discourage individual conversions. A man who feels that he has exhausted the spiritual resources of Anglicanism has no choice but to seek his nourishment elsewhere. At that moment, but not before, conversion may be an obligation of conscience. To pursue rapprochements between Churches, and to accept individual conversions is therefore not contradictory. But each conversion is, by nature, a case of its own which cannot be multiplied at random.

These remarks seem evident today, and no doubt the founders of the *Association for the Promotion of Christian Unity* (APCU) had them in mind. Established in 1857 by Frederic George Lee (1832-1902), it was conceived as a prayer league for the organic reunion of the Anglican Church, the Orthodox Church, and the Church of Rome. Lee was an Anglican priest. He could be a formidable polemicist, a tender poet, or a politician wed to impossible causes, as the occasion demanded. But his views were oftentimes correct. Two Catholics, the "neo-Gothic" architect A. W. Pugin (1812-52) and Ambrose Phillips de Lisle (1809-78), were among its founders. Some Catholic priests, of whom at least one was known as a theologian at the time, Father William Lockhart (1820-92), approved its purposes and principles.

Editor of a periodical, *The Union*,[4] Lee proved himself so enthusiastic that once in a while some of his friends tried

---

[4] Called *The Union Review* since 1863.

to bring him back to his senses. The Anglican Bishop of
Brechin, Alexander Pemrose Forbes (1817-75) advised him:
"However much the good aspects of the Roman system are
to be admired, we don't improve by trying to imitate all its
little details of discipline and practice." [5] In their desire for
organic union, Lee and de Lisle naturally wanted to be looked
on favorably by Rome. Cardinal Wiseman (1802-65) was
sympathetic to the *Association,* but Henry Manning (1808-
92), who was his assistant before succeeding him in the See
of Westminster, became increasingly opposed to it. Lee was
lacking in tact. By printing letters in *The Union* that were
written by Catholic priests in bad standing with their bishops,
he laid himself open to criticism. APCU was not directly
connected with this publication, nevertheless it was because
of this totally irresponsible journalism that the Association
was condemned on September 16, 1864, in the letter of the
Holy Office *Ad Omnes Episcopos Angliae.* APCU continued,
minus its Catholic members, until 1921.

Lee was wounded but not beaten. His plans for corporate
reunion became more and more eccentric. In 1877, together
with some friends (one is tempted to call them accomplices),
he formed a semi-secret organization called the *Order of
Corporate Reunion.* His purpose was to hasten reunion. His
method was to try and reinforce Anglican orders by obtaining
ordination or consecration from Orthodox, and, if possible,
Catholic prelates. This noble and fantastic project died in its
infancy. Lee was crude enough to have himself consecrated
a bishop illegally. Apart from a small group no one took him
seriously.

Every great movement has its Don Quixote, more enthusiastic than prudent. This does not permit condemning the
movement itself. The ideal of a corporate reunion of Churches
is something other than the impossible method that Lee
preached. Lee was right, however, in having recourse to

---

[5] Quoted by H.R.T. Brandreth in *Dr. Lee of Lambeth,* 1951, p. 93.

prayer. Other heirs of the Oxford Movement carried on with the task of Catholic restoration in Anglicanism and of collective rapprochement with the Church of Rome.

This was mainly Pusey's role. Remaining faithful to the Anglican Church, he did not desire union with the Catholic Church any the less. The explanations he gave of his ideas became increasingly more precise and clear. Pusey explained himself primarily by means of three volumes that he wrote entitled *Eirenicon*. The first volume of *Eirenicon,* published in 1865, was an answer to an open letter of Manning. Pusey pleaded for more peaceful relations between Catholics and Anglicans. He asked that Anglicans give an interpretation to the Thirty-nine Articles that wouldn't clash with the Catholic conscience. He confided to Catholics that, as an Anglican, he had no difficulty accepting the dogmatic decrees of the Council of Trent. His objections were not directed at the dogmas of faith themselves, but at the popular practices of piety which had developed since the Council, and which have, in fact if not in theory, hardened the "angles" of doctrine. But these pious practices which have hardly any basis in tradition, which have to do with belief in purgatory, indulgences, and the Virgin Mary, seem, Pusey said, to have as much importance as dogmas in the current teaching absorbed from day to day by poorly educated Catholics.

Ingratitude is oftentimes the lot of peacemakers. They are misunderstood, and the result is that their efforts provoke new quarrels. Pusey's book was well received in some Catholic circles in England and elsewhere. But Newman himself misunderstood it. He answered Pusey in an ironic and somewhat humorous tone. As a matter of fact, his *Letter to Reverend Pusey* of 1866 denied the existence of incriminated practices. But to deny what others have seen is never an answer.

A second, then a third *Eirenicon* followed in 1869 and in 1870 respectively. In them Pusey clarified certain ideas that he had expressed in his first volume. Here and there he met with just about the same degree of sympathy or lack of understanding that he had before. Shortly afterwards Pusey became disheartened over it all. The idea of a council appealed to him, but he feared there would be a definition of papal infallibility. What he feared happened. Pusey believed that his efforts were destroyed by the Vatican Council. A definition is a good thing when it is needed; yet every dogmatic definition, even if circumstances demand it, digs a deeper ditch between separated Christians. It makes it more difficult for Protestants to understand the Catholic Church. Besides that, it gives the Anglicans who are closest to us the impression that we are indifferent about their efforts at rapprochement and that we make little of increasing the obstacles.

The Oxford Movement as a whole was well disposed to Rome. It has at least thought of Rome as a model to imitate if not always as a purpose for conversion. Although it has not given the same attention to Byzantium and Moscow, the "second" and "third Rome" in the history of Eastern Christianity, the Oxford Movement has not disregarded the possibility of a rapprochement with Eastern Orthodoxy.

The branch theory explicitly makes Orthodoxy one of the three branches of the one Church. Anglicanism had not paid much attention to the East since the Non-Jurors, who were in correspondence with the Eastern patriarchs and the Holy Synod of Russia between 1716 and 1724. The relations were intensified between 1830 and 1840, when a number of Anglican dignitaries visited Byzantium and Russia. The Metropolitan of Moscow, Philaret (1782-1867), was well in advance of his time as far as the ecumenical question was concerned. In his book called *Conversation between a Seeker and a Believer,* published in 1832, he refused to condemn the Churches that were separated from Orthodoxy. To be sure, for him as for the entire Orthodox tradition, Eastern Orthodoxy is the one Church of Jesus Christ. The other

Churches still belong to Christian unity in some mysterious way, however, even though they are schismatic.

If Moscow could propose such a doctrine, it was credible and somewhat probable that an attempt at union would be welcomed. William Palmer (1811-79), one of the lesser figures of the Oxford Movement, was badly mistaken when he thought this. The Holy Synod showed little patience when Palmer, on a visit to Moscow, asked to receive Holy Communion during the Orthodox Liturgy. The Russian prelates examined Palmer's faith and the documents of the Anglican Church carefully, notably the Thirty-nine Articles. They concluded that the Church of England does not teach the Orthodox faith. Therefore no intercommunion was possible. Palmer wanted to prove the contrary. He wrote a book called *The Harmony of the Anglican Doctrine with the Eastern Catholic and Apostolic Church* (1846). Unfortunately for the author, the book had a bad reception in England. Palmer finally had to join the Catholic Church. His solitary effort was not without fruits in Anglicanism, however. The *Association for the Promotion of Christian Unity* prayed for the East no less than for Rome. Many Anglicans, even apart from the Oxford Movement, devoted themselves to the study of the Eastern Churches. Since then, Anglo-Catholic interest in Orthodoxy has continued to grow.

The ecumenical problem in Anglicanism is not restricted to the Oxford Movement. Like those on the continent, the Anglican evangelicals have striven for the brotherly union of Christians, of Protestants above all. They have favored and encouraged missionary societies, youth groups, and interdenominational biblical societies. The heirs of the "Latitudinarians" of the eighteenth century mixed with the admirers of continental liberal Protestantism. Thus nineteenth century Anglicanism made its first strides towards "reunion all-round." In 1841 an agreement between Prussia and England made an unusual Anglican-Lutheran project of collaboration possible. The Church of England and the

United Church of Prussia conjointly created a bishopric of Jerusalem. The bishop, who was to be nominated alternately by the two Churches, would be charged with the spiritual care of both Lutherans and Anglicans. The English bishops, urged on by the British government, acquiesced to this extravagant plan. This helped convince Newman of the fundamentally Protestant character of the Church of England. This illegitimate project, more political than religious, was short-lived; the 1841 agreement was broken in 1886.

Outside official circles, and at the same time that the Oxford Movement was about its work, a noteworthy Anglican thinker was elaborating a theology that must have had some influence on ecumenism. This was Frederic Denison Maurice (1805-72).

Maurice believed that the English Church is the most catholic of all the Christian Churches, because its position forges Protestantism and Catholicism into one. They are the two faces of the same coin. If Catholicism keeps its distance from Protestantism, as is the case with Rome, it itself becomes anti-catholic. This summarizes the entire message of Maurice's two volumes entitled *The Kingdom of Christ* (1838). Without Catholicism, Protestantism falls into all the extremes that the Reformation Churches suffer from. Only the Church of England has followed the good path without swerving either to the right or to the left. She has perceived that "the Reformation principles are indispensable conditions for the great Catholic truths." [6] Instead of correcting the Thirty-nine Articles as was done by the Tractarians, they should be taken for what they are, the harmonious synthesis of Catholic truths and Protestant principles. Maurice wanted to show that the Church of England not only preserves the Catholic principles, but likewise those "of Quakerism, Calvinism, Lutheranism, and Unitarianism," properly understood. Christ's Church is not a system. It is a kingdom. It is the work of

---

[6] *The Kingdom of Christ,* 4th ed., 1891, vol. 2, p. 378.

the Holy Spirit, already manifested in the kingship of the Creator over the creature, and made even more evident in the kingship of Christ over believers.

Maurice did more than anyone else in the nineteenth century to unite the various Anglican theologies. He divided them into liberal, evangelical, and "high church." Each of these "parties," according to Maurice, misses its goal if it thinks that it alone possesses an "invisible equatorial line" [7] separating Catholicism and Protestantism. Having become an exclusive system, each one implicitly denies "the Church as a spiritual body having a spiritual Head." [8] In reality, Protestant and Catholic principles are equally right. On the contrary, those systems that call themselves Catholic or would like to be only Protestant are not "the extension or expansion of the principle, but its limitation and contradiction." The Anglican schools of theology become nothing but an exaggeration of correct principles. Reduced to proper proportions, they act as mutual correctives. Similarly, in the universal Church, Protestantism and Catholicism must stop looking at one another as the negation of each other. They are inseparable brothers in spite of their differences. Each one corrects the over-systematization of the other.

According to Frederic Maurice there is also a problem of Christian unity. This problem is not institutional, but spiritual. It comes from the fact that "the concept of the Church as a unified body has primarily been taught in order to show the loss in those who are separated from it." [9] Love must now take the place of hatred. The different Churches "are themselves the living parts of the divine kingdom." [10] In regard to those whom he considers schismatic, the true Christian "wants to preserve his faith from the destruction that threatens it, to unite his faith to the faith of those from whom he

---

[7] *Ibid.*, p. 406.
[8] *Ibid.*, p. 409.
[9] *Ibid.*, p. 416.
[10] *Ibid.*, p. 417.

is separated, to have them become integral members of the body." Here Maurice is speaking explicitly of the Anglican viewpoint in respect to the adherents of the English Free Churches. Actually, he describes the ecumenical attitude as it has been discovered since, rather than as it was at the time.

Maurice should be proclaimed a precursor with prophetic insight. The theology on which he bases his desire for Christian brotherhood is undoubtedly in disagreement with true Catholic tradition in more than one respect. He did not understand Catholicism well. His theology is more Protestant and less Catholic than he thinks. His concept of the Church does not place enough emphasis on its divine origin and the indispensable function of the hierarchical institution. But as a practical attitude to adopt towards other Christians, that of Maurice deserves to be recommended. The Catholic can even adopt one of Maurice's fine statements by just changing the meaning of his terms. Maurice said that we should "discern the importance of the Protestant principle, and that its true harbor is the Catholic Church." [11]

Frederic Denison Maurice did not construct a theology of Christian unity and reunion that would have satisfied a Catholic theologian. On a number of points his synthesis was also dissatisfying to Protestants having strong confessional convictions. Yet, he steered Anglicanism in a direction where the question of Christian unity became the question of ecumenism. When it came to comparing doctrines, the Oxford Movement was tempted to complacency, whereas Maurice introduced the idea of a dynamism, a common progress towards becoming one through the study of Protestant and Catholic principles.

The doctrinal and spiritual impetus that Anglicanism incited in the nineteenth century had results even in the official circle of the bishops of the Anglican Communion. The first Lambeth Conference convened in 1867. About once in every

---

[11] *Ibid.,* p. 424.

ten years since that date the Anglican bishops converge on the Lambeth palace, the London residence of the Archbishop of Canterbury. There they discuss their common problems. In 1888 the Conference studied the relations between the Anglican Church and other Churches, particularly Protestant and Orthodox. It tried to determine under what conditions a reunion of all English Protestants could be accomplished. With some modifications, it subscribed to a resolution passed in 1886 by the General Convention of the Protestant Episcopal Church of the United States, the American branch of the Anglican Communion. This resolution has become known in history as the "Lambeth Quadrilateral."

The Lambeth Quadrilateral proposes four conditions as the bases of forthcoming reunions: acceptance of Scripture, the Creeds (the Apostles' Creed and the Nicene Creed), the two sacraments of Baptism and the Eucharist, using the traditional form and matter (the words of Christ and the elements designated by Him), and finally, "the historic episcopate, adapted locally in its administrative methods to the varying needs of the nations and peoples called by God into the unity of His Church."

These principles had important consequences. Though they were modified in the course of the Lambeth Conferences that followed, they remained substantially unchanged. Thus the question of the episcopacy was put before Protestantism. Now it is evident that there would be no question of reunion with the Catholic traditions, unless the episcopate was considered to be the cornerstone of the institutional structure of the Church. One might well ask exactly what Anglicanism means by the expression "historic episcopate." The explanations given by the Anglicans vary; and one may well, therefore, entertain doubts regarding the nature of the Anglican episcopate. It has never been recognized as valid by the Catholic Church. Pope Leo XIII declared Anglican orders invalid in 1896. After hesitating for a long time, the Orthodox prelates likewise pronounced a negative judgment in the Synod of Moscow of 1948. Although it does not necessarily involve the entire Orthodox Church, this decision is well representative of Eastern thought regarding the transmission of orders and the episcopate. But in spite of that, Anglicanism's fidelity to the episcopal tradition it has inherited has made it the champion of the Catholic structure of the Church in ecumenical dialogues. This is mainly due to the Lambeth Quadrilateral.

Thus we see that the great contribution of Anglicanism to the formation of ecumenical thought has been to propose the question of Catholic unity. Protestantism properly speaking, that of the Calvinist and Lutheran Churches, is primarily directed towards Protestant unity. Certain Lutheran movements tend, at least by implication, to call for a unity which would be truly doctrinal and not just a more or less sentimental fraternity. Anglicanism has clearly considered the problem of Catholic unity. Some of its theologians have been very open about it. Others, without stating the problem precisely, have proposed a theology of Christian unity which favors Catholicism. Perhaps the Catholic will complain that Anglicans have sometimes misrepresented the true Catholic tradition in some of their writings. This is undeniable. The Catholicism that Frederic Maurice speaks of, for example, is nothing but a distorted echo of the true voice of the Catholic Church. Thus not every profession of Catholicism is the same as traditional Catholicism. The Anglican contribution towards ecumenism should be put to a critical test. Even the most severe criticism should recognize, however, that this contribution has been irreplaceable. It has made possible an ecumenism that will not be a Protestant imperialism. It has opened the way to a dialogue with the Catholic Church.

CHAPTER V

EVEN AT THE ELEVENTH HOUR

"If Christians are ever to get together, as everything invites them to do, it seems that the movement must start in the Church of England."
—Joseph de Maistre

Catholics of the nineteenth century were very concerned about the problem of Christian unity. This fact is not sufficiently recognized even among ecumenists. Of course, when we say "Catholics," it can only be a question of an elite, or rather, an avant-garde. Catholics as a whole were already well occupied with the grave social problems, political changes, and the spread of irreligion that made up a good part of the history of their century. But there were also Catholics who shared some of the Church's anxiety over Christian discords. The tradition of the seventeenth and eighteenth centuries was the same in that respect. The names of Bossuet and of Cardinal de Noailles are well known among the leading figures who called attention to Christian unity. Their example was not forgotten. Concern over Christian union spread to other countries besides France during the nineteenth century.

The dialogue that Bossuet or Cardinal de Noailles engaged in was somewhat removed from the everyday life of the Church. The relationship between Bossuet and Leibnitz on the theological level, and between de Noailles and Count Zinzendorf on the level of piety, was a kind of exchange between experts. Here and there grandiose projects of reunion were proposed. But they were too broad to be realized. The nineteenth century channeled its efforts along entirely different lines. In limiting its plans it was more realistic. By that very fact it also permitted the people of the Church to take part in a true apostolate for unity by means of prayer, study, and example.

A possible reunion between Canterbury and Rome was in the air at the beginning of the nineteenth century. There were representatives of the "High Church" theology who dreamed of Catholic reunion even before the Oxford Movement. The Anglican Bishop of Durham, Shute Barrington (1734-1826), spoke of it in a pastoral letter in 1810. In 1818 the rector of a London parish, Samuel Wix (1771-1861), asked that a council of the two Churches make preparations for a reconciliation.

On the Catholic side, an Irish bishop opened the first modern ecumenical concern by a letter that is remarkable from all points of view. In 1824 James Warren Doyle (1786-1834), Bishop of Kildare and Leighlin, sent a message to the Chancellor of the Exchequer of the British Government. In it he stated the religious problems of Ireland, divided between the Catholic Church, which was poor but popular, and the Anglican Church, which was the official Church but the Church of a minority. Then he proposed that the position of the two Churches be consolidated by uniting them. The bishop was not thinking that this could be accomplished by a governmental decree. All he wanted was that the government support the idea of holding theological talks in view of resolving the differences between the two Churches.

The passage referring to these differences is worth quoting in full:

"The chief points to be discussed are the canon of the Sacred Scriptures, faith, justification, the Mass, the sacraments, the authority of tradition, of councils, of the Pope, the celibacy of the clergy, language of the liturgy, invocation of saints, respect for images, prayers for the dead. On most of these it appears to me there is no essential difference between the Catholics and Protestants; the existing diversity of opinions arises, in most cases, from certain forms of words which admit of satisfactory explanation, or from the ignorance and misconceptions which ancient prejudice and ill-will produce and strengthen, but which could be removed; they are pride and points of honor which keep us divided on many subjects, not a love of Christian humility, charity and truth." [1]

Not content with suggesting theological discussions, the Bishop of Kildare even suggested renouncing his episcopal see "without pay, pension, fee, or ambition," [2] if this could help towards union.

This letter indicates three points which the Catholic ecumenists were due to rediscover since then. Doyle had a presentiment of something that the long experience of ecumenical dialogues has effectively demonstrated.

In the first place, he says that most of the differences between Catholicism and Protestantism are not differences in faith. They are variations of language or misunderstandings resulting from different ways of feeling. But this is one of the conclusions reached by ecumenists today. Without denying or minimizing the doctrinal contradictions, they evaluate the vast field of non-theological factors of disunion that encumber the ecumenical problem and poison the relations of one Church with another.

In the second place the Bishop of Kildare proposes the

---

[1] H. N. Oxenham: *An Eirenicon of the 18th century,* 1879, p. 325.
[2] *Ibid.,* p. 323.

dialogue method as a remedy for this situation. The atmosphere can be cleared up only by getting together and talking things over. Explanations will make their respective vocabularies understandable. Gradually this will make it possible to speak a common theological language. Only then will it be possible to approach the ultimate dogmatic questions with results. This is precisely where one of the central issues of present-day ecumenism lies. The dialogue method alone is capable of surmounting the difficulties of communication between Catholics and Protestants. "Dialogue" is the ecumenical method par excellence. It proceeds from a mutual study of doctrines, liturgies, and sensibilities.

In the third place, the spiritual problem should be faced. Pride and matters of honor show up in the way that separated Christians behave toward each other. The solution to the essential problems will be overlooked to the extent that we are proud about what separates us. This idea approaches the concept of spiritual emulation that has recently been suggested. Before reuniting we should get together in the common love of Christ. First of all, everyone must develop in himself "a love for Christian humility, charity, and truth."

James Warren Doyle's letter had little effect. Neither Anglicans nor Catholics were interested as a group. Doyle was a pioneer in this matter, and pioneers are often poorly understood. Prophets are not always listened to. But if Doyle's proposals had been heeded, the ecumenical movement would be a hundred years in advance of its actual condition, at least as far as Catholics are concerned.

In regard to Ireland, it should be observed that the flame of Christian brotherhood that Doyle spoke of has not been sparked. Ireland, politically torn until recent years, has been pointed out as being singularly ˙ fortunate in its rapport among Christians. They have not degenerated into a shameful rivalry. The Irish Catholics could no doubt be reproached with keeping too much aloof from their Anglican and Protestant compatriots, but they have wisely averted the religious rivalries that other countries have suffered. In 1867 Bishop David Moriarty (1814-77), Bishop of Kerry, praised the Protestant clergy before his priests: "In every relation of life," he wrote, "the Protestant clergy are not only blameless, but estimable and edifying. . . . Sometimes, when we notice that quiet, and decorous, and moderate course of life, we. feel ourselves giving expression to the wish, *talis cum sis utinam noster esses.*" [3]

The question of Church union is prominent in England because of the Oxford Movement. We have seen how a number of Catholics, following the example of Ambrose Phillips de Lisle, participated in the *Association for the Promotion of Christian Union* until its condemnation by the Holy Office in 1864. Cardinal Wiseman, Archbishop of Westminster, was not personally opposed to the idea of corporate reunion. Newman, while not having much faith in it after his conversion, didn't want to do anything that might thwart the efforts of Anglicans who were working towards this end. We know that he himself was disturbed over the deplorable results that individual conversions risked in terms of the movement towards organic union.

Manning, who succeeded Wiseman in the See of Westminster, and who in turn became a cardinal, took an entirely different attitude. He was himself a product of the Oxford Movement, though never a leader in it, but he had very little regard for his former Church. On the contrary, he said that: "Far from being a defense against irreligion, the Church of England must be recognized as the mother of all the intellectual and spiritual aberrations that cover the face of England today." [4] With such an interpretation of Anglicanism Manning evidently could not tolerate the idea of corporate reunion. He tried his best to reveal this monstrous motherhood of the Anglican Church. He was at least partly responsible

---

[3] "Such as you are, I wish you were one of us." Quoted in Stephen Neill, *Anglicanism*, 1958, p. 294.

[4] *Workings of the Holy Spirit in the Church of England*, 1861, in *England and Christendom*, 1867, p. 115.

for the fact that British Catholicism, which was agreeable to
the idea of Christian reunion during the first half of the nineteenth century, tended to stand aloof from the problems of
ecumenism after that. The continuation of the dialogue with
the Anglicans was assured by Catholics on the European
continent.

The Vatican Council inspired great hopes in some Anglican circles. The definition of papal infallibility, on the other
hand, aroused disappointment. Pusey saw it as the defeat
of his own efforts and became discouraged. Lacking the
understanding of it that we enjoy today, he interpreted the
definition as the total victory of Ultramontanism, represented
in England by Cardinal Manning. He could hardly realize
that the guarantees surrounding the infallibility of the successor of St. Peter prevent it from becoming the mechanical
instrument that William Ward (1812-82) was thinking of
when he expected to get a new definition of faith with his
breakfast every morning. Be that as it may, the Anglicans
were in no position to appreciate a definition which they had
ardently hoped would not get a majority vote in the Council.
The Scottish Anglican Bishop Alexander Forbes stopped his
ecumenical activities after the definition. The discourage-
ment of great souls who had taken heart in the union ideal is
one of the unhappy spectacles of this epoch. Gerard Cobb,
an Anglican layman, the author of numerous works on the
need for reunion with Rome, had put his fondest hopes in
the Vatican Council. The definition of infallibility caused him
to lose heart. He not only abandoned his literary activity on
the part of the union, but despaired of Christianity itself. He
was the author of a book on the Eucharist and never approached the Holy Table again. What dark nights he must
have endured! Perhaps many others, whose names are not
recorded in history, have been in the same situation.

By Divine Providence these sufferings were not in vain.
The idea of a reunion between the Church of England and
the Catholic Church was soon on the rebound. On the Anglican side, this renewal was again the work of the Oxford

Movement. The men of the first generation of this catholicizing renewal had figured mostly before 1870. The Vatican
Council and the definition of papal infallibility took place
later, when they were already old men and it was difficult
for them to adjust themselves to a new situation. After 1870
their successors no longer fed the immoderate hopes of old.
They were younger, but not having experienced the extraordinary renewal that newborn Anglo-Catholicism had enjoyed, they were less impatient with the innumerable delays
that every movement of Christian reunion encounters. At
this time a section of Anglo-Catholicism even became greatly
disinterested in the question. Anglo-Catholicism as such became more independent of pro-Roman tendencies. The course
followed by the Anglo-Catholic left wing can be seen in *Lux
Mundi* (1889), which was the work of theologians grouped
around Charles Gore (1853-1932).

Roman union continued to preoccupy other minds. Charles
Lindley Wood, later known by his title of Lord Halifax
(1839-1934), made a fresh attempt. This time it wasn't the
work of Anglicans alone. They were aided by Catholics, especially by the French Vincentian Fernand Portal (1855-
1926). Fernand Portal and Lord Halifax had met in 1890 on
the Isle of Madeira. Portal went there for his health, and
Halifax was there with his own son who was severely ill. The
two men got along together admirably. They collaborated
until their death in an effort to prepare people's minds for a
future organic reunion that would be realized when God
willed it.

The facts are well known. Portal and Halifax wanted to
make the Anglican question known among Catholics. They
decided to bring up the problem of Anglican orders again.
Under the pseudonym Fernand Dalbus, Portal published a
series of articles in which he concluded that Anglican orders
were invalid. He did not fail to attract the attention of intel-
lectuals. Abbé Louis Duchesne (1843-1922), using the same
documents, came to the opposite conclusion. Other professors

in Paris set themselves to studying Anglican orders, among them being Abbé Auguste Boudinhon (1858-1941) and Bishop Pietro Gasparri (1852-1934), who was teaching at the Catholic Institute at that time. Duchesne and Boudinhon became celebrated Church historians. Gasparri, a great Italian canonist, later received the cardinal's hat and became Vatican Secretary of State under Benedict XV and Pius XI. Portal's writings came to the attention of the Holy See. Called to Rome for consultation, Abbé Portal asked Pope Leo XIII to make a conciliatory gesture toward the Anglicans. After receiving Halifax in audience, Leo XIII published the apostolic letter *Amantissimae voluntatis* on April 14, 1895, which he addressed "to the English who desire the kingship of Christ in the unity of faith." The letter did not speak of "submission" but of "reconciliation and peace." He encouraged a patient search for unity. Here the question of union was considered solely from the overall point of view, with no mention of individual conversions.

This initial success encouraged Halifax and Portal to continue with their efforts towards collective rapprochements. In December, 1895, Portal founded the *Anglo-Roman Review* in Paris. The question of Anglican ordinations was raised at Rome. Leo XIII realized the advantages of a judgment that would be acceptable to the Anglicans. Just the same, acting on the justifiable entreaties of Cardinal Herbert Vaughan (1832-1903), Archbishop of Westminster, he decided not to depart from the practice of the Church without extensive study. Now since the end of the sixteenth century the Church had treated Anglican orders as invalid. Therefore a historical commission was charged with studying the documents anew.[5] While the Commission was at work, the Holy Father pub-

---

[5] The members of the Commission were Dom Aidan Gasquet, Canon Moyes, Father David Fleming, O.F.M., who opposed validity, and Bishop Gasparri, Abbé Duchesne, and Father de Augustinis, S.J., who favored validity. Two other members were added later, Father Scannell and Father Calasanzio de Lleveneras, O.F.M.C.

lished his encyclical letter on the unity of the Church, *Satis cognitum* (June 29, 1896). A short time after this the Commission for the Study of Anglican Orders finished its work. The individual judgments of its members, which were submitted to the Sovereign Pontiff, naturally reflected their own opinions. As we know, they went in opposite directions. Their discussions resulted in a new series of conclusions. When the Holy Office was informed of the results, it advised Leo XIII. On September 13, 1896, the Pope published the bull *Apostolicae Curae,* in which he declared Anglican orders invalid. This was apparently the defeat of Portal and Halifax.

We will return later to the ecumenical doctrine of the Roman documents. What is of importance at the moment is to understand Abbé Portal's ideas.

Portal was convinced of the remote possibility of a corporate reunion. He did not expect a reunion in the near future, but thought that the Lord's hour would come only if men, Catholics and Anglicans alike, were prepared for it. They had to know each other before reuniting. The movement of the Spirit by which God will one day reunite all Christians in the one Church would not be a miracle. God will not give anyone an infused knowledge of the doctrines and sentiments of others. Thus the first step towards collective rapprochements is to know one another. Portal's initial effort then, had to do with making Anglicanism known, above all the branch that was most advanced in the direction of organic reunion, namely, Anglo-Catholicism. Abbé Portal succeeded admirably. He promoted a mutual exchange of information between Catholic and Anglican theology that has continued since. Moreover, he established important personal contacts between Anglicans and Catholics, mainly in Rome and in France. He could see no possibility of a reunion without previous friendship. And friendships between groups always begin by rapprochements among their elite.

To speak of this as "Catholic ecumenism" is undoubtedly an anachronism. However, Catholic ecumenism is essentially what Abbé Portal had in mind. Today again we enjoy a state of mutual exchange where esteem and friendship prevail. Portal is evidently the one who set things moving in this direction. In this sense he is the father of Catholic ecumenism.

No matter how enthusiastic he was about the ideal of corporate reunion, Abbé Portal proposed no set plan. He was too much of a realist for that. He was under no illusion about the chances for the success of preliminary discussions in view of an immediate reunion. The time was not ripe for discussions around a conference table but for conciliatory gestures which, while enlightening people's minds as to the necessity of peace and unity, would stir up the imagination. Today's impossibilities are just tomorrow's possibilities. This is the kind of conciliatory gesture that he suggested to Leo XIII, and that the Sovereign Pontiff himself made in his letter *Ad Anglos*.

The result of efforts made for the union of Christians has to do with faith as such. Lord Halifax, great soul that he was, wrote to Portal after the condemnation of Anglican orders: "We are momentarily defeated, but God willing, His will shall be accomplished, and if He permits us to be wounded, it is because He wants to do these things Himself. This is no dream, it is as sure as ever." [6] Abbé Portal also placed the solution to the problem of unity in the realm of faith. To desire unity is but to be faithful to the prayer of Christ: "That they may be one." It means believing in the catholicity of the Church, whose unity is not fully manifested unless it embraces the whole Christian world. Here again Portal clearly perceived the exigencies of a Catholic ecumenism. It would recognize the purpose of ecumenical effort: the reunion of all Christian Churches in the unity of the Catholic hierarchy. But he did not know by what ways God would have Christians pass before they would be thus reunited. Therefore he left the door open to individual conversions for those whose

---

[6] Quoted by Jacques de Bivort de la Saudée, *op. cit.*, p. 41.

conscience so directed them to the light, as well as to collective rapprochements, the indispensable preludes to large-scale reunions.

Thanks to the initiative of Abbé Portal, Catholic Europe was introduced to ecumenism. Catholic America in turn has in its own way followed a similar course. To be truthful, the question of Christian reunion has not been proposed to American Catholics. Recent immigrants for the most part, they have had to resolve urgent practical problems. They have had to develop the ecclesiastical organism fast enough to cope with the waves of Catholics that have converged on the United States from Germany, Italy, Poland, and above all from Ireland. Building the Church in what quickly became the forty-eight states put Catholicism in a new situation facing Protestantism. On the one hand, Catholicism was a minority, as was equally true in many parts of Europe. On the other hand, it did not influence the formation of the original United States. The thirteen states that fought the Revolution were Protestant and for the most part Puritan (i.e., Calvinist). As a result, Protestantism formed the American religious conscience, just as Catholicism had formerly formed that of Europe, even those parts of Europe that later became Protestant. Besides, American civilization, being heir to the English turn of mind, was pragmatic and empirical. It was more interested in practical problems than in speculative questions.

Thus, during the nineteenth century American Catholicism had to find a new means of coexistence with Protestantism. This was primarily the work of the great American bishops of this period. They did not face the problem in terms of Christian unity and schisms, but primarily in terms of American society, which was essentially pluralistic. How could Catholicism thrive in a society where religious pluralism is written into the very Constitution itself? The theoretical solution adopted by the majority of bishops, following the example of John England (1786-1842), Bishop of Charleston,

EVEN AT THE ELEVENTH HOUR

and later those of John Ireland (1838-1918), Archbishop of Saint Paul, and of Cardinal James Gibbons (1834-1921), Archbishop of Baltimore, was to assume religious pluralism as an exigency of the Catholic faith. The faith could flourish nowhere better than in a climate of religious freedom. The kind of religious pluralism where Churches multiply themselves and sometimes degenerate into sects is but the counterpart of freedom of belief. A surprising remark appeared in the joint pastoral letter of the Bishops of the United States in 1884 that is to be understood in this sense. "The hierarchy of the Catholic Church of the United States is convinced that the American political institutions can more easily help a man reach salvation than those of Europe."

The bishops of the past century all shared an admirably liberal viewpoint in regard to brushing shoulders with Protestants in daily life. When John England covered his immense diocese by horseback in the 1830's, he accepted invitations to preach in Protestant Churches. Since the Protestant communities were oftentimes without a pastor, they were happy to hear any traveler capable of speaking to them of God. Being involved in very complicated affairs affecting the administration of Church property, England devised the "Charleston Constitution" for his diocese. It gave rights to the Catholic laity that it has never enjoyed anywhere else. His system, which was similar to that which prevailed in the Anglican Church in the United States, made Catholic diocesan life very much like Anglican diocesan life in certain respects. Every year, from 1823 to 1842, the date of England's death, an "assembly" brought together the two "chambers" made up of the clergy and the lay delegates of the diocese. The temporal administration of the Church was the main job of this assembly.

England, moreover, was not the only one who took an intelligent interest in the problems peculiar to American Catholics. William Clancy, his coadjutor for some years, launched a remarkable appeal for solidarity among Christians when

cholera ravaged the Carolinas in 1836: "Let Catholics, Epis-
copalians, Methodists, Presbyterians, Universalists, Baptists,
and all other denominations learn, even at the eleventh hour,
to look on each other as brethren of one common social family, and combine in the enviable occupation of doing mutual
good, and avoiding all moral and physical evil." [7]

The adaptation of the Church to American religious pluralism reached its zenith in 1894. Following the universal exposition in Chicago in 1892, a world congress of religions,
rather inappropriately styled the "Parliament of Religions,"
was organized. This Congress was convoked in 1893. The
Catholic Church was invited. The two archbishops, Gibbons
and Ireland, attended the "Parliament" themselves. Under
the direction of Monsignor John Keane (1823-1918), rector
of Catholic University in Washington, twenty lecturers spoke
between September 11-28, 1893. They explained to their
audience to the best of their ability how the Church wished
to serve humanity. This was the general theme of the Congress.

No ecumenical theory animated this participation in the
Chicago Congress. Rather, it was an occasion for American
Catholicism to present itself to the public of its land, and to
take part in a cultural manifestation of American pluralism.
Such a participation would not have been possible without
considerable open-mindedness. This very trait is seen in one
of the great American Catholics of this epoch. Father Isaac
Hecker (1819-88), a former agnostic who became a Catholic, saw the Church as the crown of the religious pluralism
of his country. She was the providential end towards which
all the Churches of the United States are on the march, and
which they will one day join. But one condition would have
to be fulfilled in order for this program of union to be realized; the Church must truly show itself to Americans as being
established on the foundation of freedom of belief. Thus

---

[7] Peter Guilday, *The Life and Times of John England,* vol. 2,
1927, p. 340-1.

Hecker offered a theological justification for religious pluralism which contained, in principle, the ecumenical program.

The mistake of youth, which is also the mistake of men,
of nations, and even of Churches, is oftentimes to be in too
much of a rush. Ireland, Gibbons, and Hecker, like their
predecessor England, had enemies who hurried them. When
faced with internal dissensions, Rome always takes the path
of sound prudence. After England's death the Charleston
Constitution, which no other bishop cared to adopt, ceased
to function. In 1896 Monsignor Keane, who had organized
the participation in the Parliament of Religions, was relieved
of his post at Catholic University. In 1899 the apostolic
letter of Leo XIII, *Testem benevolentiae,* condemned "Amer-
icanism." This expression included the enthusiasm for religious pluralism that Ireland had shown, as well as a certain
number of ideas on modern spirituality that were no doubt
mistakenly attributed to Hecker. This matter has been referred to as a phantom heresy. Some authors have attributed
to the intervention of *Testem benevolentiae* the fact that there
is no modernism in the Church of the United States. Be that
as it may, the year 1899 marked the end of this first American contribution to the birth of Catholic ecumenism.

Without dealing with the ecumenical problem as such,
American Catholics had arrived at a conclusion that implied
an ecumenical attitude. The problem, for them, was sociological. But it occasioned theological postulates on freedom of
belief that are to be found at the basis of any Catholic ecumenism. The American bishops saw rightly that religious
pluralism within a country can constitute a guarantee of
freedom for the faith, and consequently, for sincere adherence to Catholicism. They were not so fully aware of the fact
that, even in a democratic pluralism, pressures of all sorts
can likewise make Catholicism a social convention rather
than a spiritual conviction. Nevertheless, their acceptance of
the principle of religious pluralism is the foundation of Catholic ecumenism, which breaks forth as soon as this same

principle is applied to the faith of Protestants, Anglicans, and the Orthodox. The freedom of their act of faith and their sincere adherence to Christ calls for a friendly attitude towards them on our part. Recognition of their freedom as men and freedom of belief are preliminary to the mutual understanding that must precede collective rapprochements.

CHAPTER VI

UNITY IN THE CHURCH

"A hope that forces itself more and more on every Ger-
man acquainted with the history of his country is that
reconciliation will be brought about where the schism
was born, and that a higher and better unity will be
born from the very same womb that gave birth to the
division."

—Ignatius von Döllinger

The different situations in America and in Europe show that ecumenical development does not follow a single pattern. Catholicism is capable of welcoming ecumenism whenever there are rapprochements of thought between Catholics and other Christians. This, in effect, was the case with England and France in the course of events mentioned in the previous chapter. Catholicism can work with the Protestant Churches or even with non-Christian religions whenever outstanding social problems demand it. This was the case in America.

German Catholicism was equally open to ecumenism during the nineteenth century. It followed a course that was suited to itself and that cannot be compared with the paths that the French and the Americans had taken. This new path consisted in the theological revival of the School of Tübingen.

At the beginning of the last century, German Catholicism set about extricating itself from a certain decadence. Following the great effort of the Counter-Reformation, it had partially lost its vitality during the Age of Enlightenment. Its theological schools had fallen under the influence of eighteenth century rationalism. Due mainly to the great Michael Sailer (1751-1832), Bishop of Ratisbon, the pastoral office was resuscitated at the beginning of the nineteenth century. Subsequently theology itself recovered.[1]

This renewal was almost entirely the work of Johann Adam Moehler (1796-1838). A professor of church history at Tübingen, then at Munich, Moehler and more than anyone else to bring German theology back to the Fathers of the Church. Under the influence of the masters at Tübingen, themselves disciples of Sailer, young Moehler was introduced to problems of Church renewal. Following the advice of his professors, he was able to make the rounds of the German universities, Protestant as well as Catholic. He saw with his own eyes the religious renewal wrought by Schleiermacher in Berlin. The result of this initiation and of his intensive study of the Fathers of the Church was the first major development of what might be called a theology of ecumenism.

Moehler first became known as a theologian through a book on the subject of unity, *Unity in the Church, or the Principle of Catholicism in the Spirit of the Fathers of the First Three Centuries of the Church* (1825). The theology of his day suffered from a false traditionalism. Its various forms, as represented by George Hermes (1775-1831), professor at Bonn, Louis Bautain (1782-1854), professor at Strasbourg, and Felicité de Lammenais (1782-1854), were condemned by the Church. Nevertheless, in 1825 Hermes still triumphed in Germany, and the Archbishop of Cologne made him his favorite theologian.

---

[1] Friedrich Wilhelm Kant-Zeubach, *Johann Michael Sailer und der ökumenische Gedanke*, 1955.

Moehler broke directly with the method that rationalized the faith. He saw the work of the Holy Spirit as being at the heart of the Church's unity. "By means of this presence of the Holy Spirit, the assembly of all the faithful, that is to say, of the Church, has now become the inexhaustible treasure, the unceasing spring, the ever-renewing youth, the new principle of life, the superabundant nourishment that is offered to all." [2] The Holy Spirit renews the face of the earth by means of the Church. The unity of the Church is none other than the unity of the Spirit in the hearts of Christians. This unity manifests itself in the unanimity of its teaching. The Spirit diffuses within hearts what He causes to be known in an external way by means of the believers' words. Unanimous doctrine is the external sign of the Spirit. The Church was recognized by this unanimity. Heresy, which denies unanimity, thereby rejects the Spirit. If the Church is an institution, she is above all "an effect of the Christian faith, the result of the living love of the faithful brought together by means of the Holy Spirit." [3]

If Moehler thinks of the Church primarily in terms of the Spirit communicated and present to the Christian multitude, he does not disregard the hierarchic unity of the faithful. Like unity of doctrine, this is a sign of the presence of the Spirit. The bishop himself constitutes this sign of the Spirit. Moehler saw him as "common love personified, and the center of everything." [4] There is an exchange of love between the bishop and his people. This is what unity consists in. The bishop is "in the community and the community is in him." [5] Unity in the Spirit is dynamic, and unity in the episcopate is an organic unity. Many bishops are united in their metropolitan. All are united in the universal episcopate, whether together in council or not. The universal episcopate is united

---

[2] *L'Unité dans l'Eglise* (coll. *Unam Sanctam*), 1938, p. 8.
[3] *Ibid.*, p. 161.
[4] *Ibid.*, p. 172.
[5] *Ibid.*, p. 173.

in its primate, the Bishop of Rome, who is "a personified reflection of the unity of the whole Church." [6]

Another key principle in Moehler's theology was the concept of the Church as an active force. Interior unity in the Spirit would be manifest in the exterior unity of the episcopate. This led Moehler to study the condition of separated Christians. In the face of such a concept of unity, the existence of Christians separated from the episcopate seemed like a scandal. It is an intolerable paradox, because it seems to contradict the fundamental principle of the relationship between the unity of the Spirit in the hearts of the faithful and the visible unity of the hierarchy. This problem is not considered in *Unity in the Church,* but is taken up in *Symbolism,* or *Exposition of the Doctrinal Differences between Catholics and Protestants* (1832). This book has something very important to say from the very start; it is not simply a comparative study. Moehler does not content himself with reviewing the various doctrines or arranging a catalogue of errors followed by their refutation. He studies Protestantism because of its connections with the Church.

Unity in the Church describes a dynamic unity that includes all differences and has an affinity with all. "The Church," Moehler says, "formed the unconscious unity of all heresies before their break and their conscious unity after their break. In the course of the break she was opposed to them all, as they were towards one another." [7] Heresy takes up a theological distinction maintained by the Church. Cutting its ties with unity, it transforms the distinction into an antithesis. Thus heresy constitutes a half-truth, becomes off-centered because it is not better connected with the center. Its rapport with the Church is at an end. To whatever extent it remains capable of rejoining the Church, it maintains a potential rapport with her that can be actualized in the future.

---

[6] *Ibid.,* p. 220.
[7] *Ibid.,* p. 148.

An analogous point of view is expressed by *Symbolism*. The Church is a doctrinal synthesis. Protestantism, monopolizing a number of Catholic truths and separating them from the rest, is an antithesis. For the sake of argument, Catholicism would then appear as the thesis. In itself, it remains the synthesis into which the thesis and antithesis must be resolved. It is no thesis except in exercising an opposition to Protestantism. It follows that the antithesis should be referred to in order to understand the thesis. And the antithesis does not make sense except in relation to the thesis. "The Catholic thesis must be placed parallel to the Protestant antithesis and must be compared with it in every point if the latter is to be well understood. Besides, Catholic doctrine does not show up in its true light except when faced with Protestant doctrine." [8]

Moehler did not develop all these implications from the ecumenical point of view, nevertheless this is well within the field of ecumenism. Protestantism is a mistake. But this mistake enjoys an eminently positive role in bringing about rapport with the Church; it puts its doctrine in its true light. This light shows precisely that the doctrinal unity of Catholicism preserves a sound balance among elements of divergent tendencies. "Real differences," says Moehler, "are possible only in unity." [9] Thus there is a relationship between the various Protestant Churches or doctrines and the various aspects of Catholicism. "As the Church includes all the differences within its unity, and as it is one, so it follows that it has an affinity with all." [10] The differences arising from the antitheses abandon Catholic unity. But the antithesis that has become Protestantism is germane to the difference existing within Catholic unity and is but an exaggeration of it.

---

[8] These quotations from *Symbolism* are taken from the following English translation: *Symbolism, or Exposition of the Doctrinal Differences between Catholics and Protestants,* translated by J. B. Robertson, New York, 1906; quotation, p. 3.

[9] *L'Unité dans l'Eglise,* p. 146.

[10] *Ibid.,* p. 168.

There might be a way of building on this basis a theory of the agreements that subsist between Catholicism and Protestantism despite their differences. Only the real Catholic understands the depths of Protestantism. An ethics of practical relations between Catholics and Protestants can be deduced from this theory. The Catholic must learn from the Protestant what great truths of Church tradition the latter holds. Such relations, that may be called dialectical, inspire a friendly attitude. This is the unifying centre of contemporary ecumenism. Basically, all of modern Catholic ecumenism is formulated in Moehler's work.

Moehler utilizes a strictly objective method for studying Protestant doctrines. He tries to understand them, therefore he describes the genesis of Protestant thought. His purpose is to make Protestantism and Catholicism known through each other. Still, he wants to know Protestantism as Protestants themselves experience it. Feeling that he might substitute ideas which are sometimes hardly representative of this or that Protestant theologian in place of Protestantism itself, he avoids centering his study around the various kinds of Lutheran or Calvinist theology. Rather, he gives his attention to some general typical characteristics. His own theology is representative of no particular school; he aims at following the consensus of the Fathers and the Councils. At the same time, his exposition of Protestantism gives first place to the confessional books and official professions of faith. This guarantee of objectivity shows that he is anxious to be intellectually honest. This is not said to exaggerate Moehler's importance, but to show that he initiated a new method of study and of ecumenical research. Moehler himself clearly outlined it in the preface to *Symbolism:* "It seems to me that a real end to the differences that separate Christian communities is still a far way off. But by publishing a true exposition of the big dispute I have hoped to be able to do something with a view to furthering religious peace, and this

will be realized to the extent that this exposition makes us
see that this dispute is born of a profound desire on both
sides to defend the truth, to defend pure and authentic
Christianity in all its integrity." [11]

This anxiety to discover the true spiritual meaning of
Protestantism must be considered in the light of Moehler's
personal experience. In the course of his rounds of the German universities, he did not conceal his admiration for certain
Protestant masters that he had occasion to hear. Direct
contact with men is rather indispensable to a true understanding of their doctrines. In our day it is impossible to
know the reformers except through their writings. But this
reading is seen in a new light if we have direct contact with
their disciples. The experience of Protestant life obtained by
close association with separated Christians is indispensable
to understanding the doctrines in their living context.

Today's reader will see the evidence of these remarks if
he is at all familiar with Catholic literature on ecumenism.
He is accustomed to an objective and respectful method of
research, and is rather surprised when he reads a supposedly
serious study of Protestantism which treats the subject in
an offhand manner, without the exact rigor of modern historical methods. But it is not always possible to get ideas across
this way. To evaluate Moehler's importance in this initiation
to the objective study of Protestantism, it suffices to compare
his *Symbolism* with another work that appeared at the same
time.

A well-known Spanish author, Jaime Balmes (1810-48),
published four volumes in 1841, 1842, 1843 and 1844
called *Protestantism Compared with Catholicism*. His purpose was to refute a book written by the French Protestant
François Guizot (1787-1874), and to prove the superiority
of Catholicism over Protestantism by comparing their influence
on society. Balmes' thesis, contrary to Guizot's, is that Prot-

---

[11] *Ibid.*, p. XVI.

estantism corrupts, while Catholicism develops all the social virtues.

Whatever value this thesis may have, a value that may be questioned, Balmes took the reverse of Moehler's position from the very start. Contrary to the German theologian, the Spanish philosopher denied the very possibility of studying Protestant doctrines. "In fact," he wrote, "if you want to attack Protestantism in its doctrines, you do not know where to turn, because you never know what the doctrines are, and Protestantism itself ignores the fact. You might say that Protestantism is invulnerable in this respect, since what is without a body is invulnerable." [12]

It would be unjust to judge Balmes solely from an ecumenical point of view, because that was not the perspective he had in mind. Balmes wrote a very scholarly apologetical and polemical work. He was one of the great minds of nineteenth century Spanish Catholicism. But as far as the study of Protestantism is concerned, his method did not measure up to his genius. He lived in a different world from that of Moehler.

Moehler's innovation does not lose any of its impact if we take a look at his predecessors. Some serious studies of Protestantism were made before his time. Francisco Suarez (1548-1616), Robert Bellarmine (1542-1621), Bossuet (1627-1704), to mention a few great names, had written extensive controversial works that are still worth consulting. But here again they introduce us to a world other than Moehler's, namely, that of polemics. This is a polemic of the highest quality, sustained by a rigorous theological method. The only thing lacking is an effort towards interior understanding, which is the only way of seeing the meaning of doctrines.[13] Otherwise it is beyond reproach. How could we

---

[12] *El Protestantismo comparado con el Catolicismo,* in *Obras completas de Jaime Balmes,* vol. 4, Madrid, 1949, p. 16.
[13] The titles are well indicative of the controversial atmosphere: Suarez, *Défense de la foi catholique contre les erreurs de la secte*

demand that all theologians break away from historical contingencies, and escape the social pressures of their day? Nobody who undertakes theological research would dare make such a demand.

The ecumenism implied in Moehler's theology becomes even more evident if we notice its relationship with the theology of certain Orthodox thinkers of his time. While Moehler was working on his books, the Russian Alexis Khomiakov (1804-60) was preparing to launch the Slavophil movement. Aside from his conviction that he had a key to the history of the world, there is little that would make Khomiakov figure in a study of ecumenism properly so-called. It will suffice to call attention to one point.

Khomiakov's ecclesiology, like that of Moehler, is an ecclesiology of the Holy Spirit. There is no sentimentality in it, since the love that makes the Church and on which it lives is the Holy Spirit Himself. Schisms and heresies are rejections of love, first of all, a fact that is illustrated by the self-exile of the schismatic or heretic from the body of believers. This is how Khomiakov understands the catholicity *(sobornost)* of Orthodoxy, which puts unanimity before universality.

Moehler is not directly concerned with the Orthodox problem. He excused himself for this in the opening pages of *Symbolism,* reasoning that there was little interest in the differences between East and West. "The fact is that there is no interest nowadays in turning towards the Eastern Church and its tributaries, for although the old feud between these communities and the Catholic and Protestant Churches still exists, it does not have any really vital influence at present." [14] If Moehler had not died so young, he would undoubtedly have taken account of the genuine interest that

---

anglicane (1612); Bellarmine, *Disputations sur les controverses de la foi chrétienne contre les hérétiques de ce temps* (1626); Bossuet, *Histoire des variations des Eglises protestantes* (1688).

[14] *Ibid.*, p. 3.

Eastern theology always presents. His concern about a patristic theology brought him very close to the Orthodox turn of mind. Actually, there could be no better way of approaching Orthodoxy than by starting out with Moehler's theology.

Moehler's thought might also be related to that of another Russian theologian, Vladimir Soloviev (1853-1900). Soloviev was acquainted with Moehler's work and referred to it occasionally. His study of unity led to his writing *Russia and the Universal Church* (1889).

Soloviev conceived the universal Church as the unifying center of the human race restored through love. The Church is established on "the truth of the God-man, that is, on the perfect and living unity of the absolute and the relative, of the infinite and the finite, of the Creator and the creature." [15] In the Church, each believer is united to the others through love. This calls for a hierarchy centered in a primacy. "Though the unity of the whole is not immediately manifested by each, it must be effected by means of the individual." [16] As with Moehler, the hierarchy is a dynamic element immediately ordered to the unity of the Church. "The formal character of truth is to order the multiple elements of the real into a harmonious unity. It possesses truth par excellence, the truth of the God-man, who, in His absolute unity, embraces the entire fullness of divine and human life. The Church, a gathering that aspires to perfect unity, must correspond to Christ, who is one being and the center of all beings." [17] From here Soloviev draws his conclusion that there is no unity today without the Bishop of Rome. "Universal truth perfectly realized in one person, Christ, brings with it a faith infallibly determined for all by one person, the Pope." [18] As Soloviev understood it, the unity

---

[15] *La Russie et l'Eglise Universelle,* 3rd ed., 1922, p. 114.
[16] *Ibid.,* p. 119.
[17] *Ibid.,* p. 118-9.
[18] *Ibid.,* p. 119.

of the universal Church is common to Catholicism and to Orthodoxy. In spite of the schism that separates them, they are united in love and in truth. The Pope is the symbol and cornerstone of this unity.

During his sojourn in Tübingen, Moehler was in friendly relations with another Church historian, Ignatius von Döllinger (1799-1890). Döllinger, who outlived Moehler by fifty years, became the leading figure in the Old Catholic schism. Refusing to recognize the doctrinal infallibility of the Bishop of Rome after the Vatican Council, Döllinger, with a following of German and Swiss priests and laymen, contacted the old Jansenist Church of Utrecht, which had gone into schism in the seventeenth century. The old Dutch group and the new German and Swiss groups united to form the Old Catholic Church.

Döllinger, however, had a deep interest in Christian unity. His strange destiny was to start another cleavage. But he tried to turn the evil into good. He wanted to make this Church that pretended to be the ancient Catholic Church the center of universal Christian reunion. "The time is coming," Döllinger wrote in 1872, "if, as many think, it has not already come, when the Church of Peter and the Church of Paul will become the Church of John, and as they said in the middle ages, when the age of the Father and the age of the Son will be succeeded by the age of the Holy Spirit." [19] Döllinger was directing this remark towards the Orthodox Churches and the Roman Catholic Church, but he did not exclude any Church from the effort to recover the unity that had been broken. With a vision that was ahead of his time, he asked all Churches to put themselves at each other's service: "Let the various Churches share their understanding and privileges in common. This would be community of goods in the highest sense." [20] Condemning schism as a "great

---

[19] *La Réunion des Eglises,* tr. by Mme. Loyson, 1880, p. 12.
[20] *Ibid.,* p. 12.

sin," [21] Döllinger disclosed vast prospects for the missionary possibilities of the one Church. Let divided Christian bodies be sent out to preach the Gospel. Thus Döllinger already recommended something that the Protestant missionary movement was about to take up.

The obstacles will be great. "For two Churches to be able to unite, they must be dominated by a spirit of union such as has rarely been found in history." [22] Thus Döllinger was looking for signs of the future in the various parts of the Christian world. Deeply moved, he concluded: "Where there are faith and love there surely is hope. Whoever believes in Christ, who loves his country and his brethren of all denominations, cannot give up hope that in the near future there will be one Church that will be the heir and lawful representative of the primitive Church, and which will be able to include and receive into its bosom all who are now separated." [23] No doubt Döllinger is often mistaken in his prophecies. In his lectures on the reunion of Churches, he affirmed that the Catholic youth of Germany would never accept the dogma of papal infallibility. This rejection would mark the return of Roman Catholic Germans to Old Catholicism, and this in turn would be a prelude to universal reunion. This pleasant illusion is completely shattered, but if Döllinger's objections to infallibility and his "anti-Jesuit" obsession are hardly of any interest, his hope for Christian unity, even though formed in the midst of a new schism, is something worthwhile.

Döllinger did not content himself with theorizing. He tried to make the Old Catholics the leaven of unity, but met with little success. The Old Catholic Congress of 1871 already passed a resolution that envisioned a reunion with the Orthodox in the near future, and a progressive rapprochement with Anglicans and Protestants. In 1874 and 1875 the Old Catholics organized meetings which would be called ecu-

---

[21] *Ibid.*, p. 13.
[22] *Ibid.*, p. 32.
[23] *Ibid.*, p. 98.

menical today. Orthodox, Anglicans, and Lutherans held
theological discussions with the Old Catholics. Other congresses were held in an attempt to prolong this initial ecumenical effort.[24] The Lucerne Congress, held in 1892,
founded a review along ecumenical lines that is still being
published.[25] The active contribution of the Old Catholics to
the ecumenical work is mostly centered in this publication
now. The Old Catholic movement has lost (supposing it ever
had it) the impetus that Döllinger dreamed of imparting to it.
His idea of establishing an association made up of Christians
of all denominations that would become the nucleus of a recovered unity, like a "snowball that would quickly become a
veritable avalanche," [26] was only a dream.

Döllinger wanted unity without the Bishop of Rome. He
was betting against the Pope, and it seems that he lost his
bet. A lesson of ecumenical importance must be learned
from the failure of the Old Catholics. There will be no
universal reunion without the Bishop of Rome, since there
can be no Catholic unity without Roman Catholicism.

Döllinger nevertheless deserves being recognized as a
pioneer of ecumenism. He was right in asking Christians to
get together and help one another before reuniting. He was
equally right in designating "Holy Scripture and the three
ecumenical Symbols drawn up by the Church in the first
centuries" [27] as the point of departure in the move towards
unity. This is undoubtedly incomplete. What his friend
Moehler brought to light should be added: the early Church
is known only by virtue of the Spirit of the Lord manifesting
Himself today. The Spirit that formerly guided the Church
still guides it. A Catholic reunion must recognize the permanent infallibility of the Church, which is the Body of Christ
and the Spouse of the Holy Spirit.

---

[24] The principal Old Catholic Congresses were held annually from
1871 to 1875, then in 1880 and 1892.

[25] *Internationale Theologische Zeitschrift,* later called *Internationale Kirchlische Zeitschrift.*

[26] *Ibid.,* p. 157.

[27] *Ibid.,* p. 157.

CHAPTER VII

ROMA LOCUTA EST

*"If it could be truly said that we were pushing towards
the coming of the time promised by God when there
will be but one flock and one shepherd, then we would
arrive at the complete fulfillment of our desires."*
—Leo XIII

The Catholic Church paid a great deal of attention to the
problems of Christian reunion during the second half of the
nineteenth century. We have cited the writings and activities
of certain theologians. We should likewise take account of
the numerous official documents issued by the hierarchy of
the Church. A recent ecumenical study connected with the
pontifical documents has been able to refer to no less than
thirty-five encyclicals or letters published by Leo XIII alone
during the twenty-five years of his reign (1878-1903).[1]
Not all of them deal explicitly with this subject. Some only
make brief references to it. Taken as a whole, however, these
documents contain a coherent and rich doctrine on the state
of Christians separated from the Roman Communion, and

---

[1] See Gregory Baum, *That They May Be One; A Study of Papal
Doctrine, Leo XIII-Pius XII*, 1958.

on the attitude that Catholics have towards them. The papal writings should not be expected to give an exhaustive treatment of the ecumenical question. They are usually timely writings published in view of some particular circumstances or to celebrate some feast or jubilee. They presume that the general state of affairs and the principal points of doctrine are known. Staying within this traditional framework, they bring up some point or other, calling attention to the opportunity of some particular consideration, or bringing some teaching to mind. So they must be read in reference to the common teaching that they usually expound.

In reading the encyclicals and other pontifical or episcopal writings, two dangers must be avoided. On the one hand, the papal teachings must be recognized for what they really are, as formulating the ordinary magisterium of the Church. Their importance must not be minimized under the pretext that they are rather brief. On the other hand, they should not be made more important than they are, and read as if they all contained the infallible definitions of faith coming from the extraordinary magisterium of the Church. The ordinary magisterium of the bishops and the Pope certainly involves an infallible teaching. This is the case when it deals directly with revealed truth, with the guarantee that the unanimity of the hierarchical teaching furnishes. More often however, the ordinary magisterium contents itself with recalling certain principles which it proceeds to apply to a concrete situation, following the dictates of practical wisdom. Infallibility would be entirely unnecessary in this case. Besides, it would not be at all in conformity with the definition of infallibility given by the Vatican Council.

These remarks can be applied right here. The first two documents to be considered date from the pontificate of Pius IX. One is the letter of the Holy Office of September 16, 1864, *Ad omnes episcopos Angliae,* condemning Catholic participation in the *Association for the Promotion of Christian Unity.* A Communication of November 8, 1865, signed by Cardinal Patrizi should be added to this. These letters publish a restrictive decision pertaining to a local situation. They make no pretense of stating the absolute norms of Catholic ecumenism. It would be a clear exaggeration to claim to find in them "universal and eternal principles," "covering practically all the major phases of the ecumenical problem." [2] If that were the case, we would be compelled to say that there is no such thing as Catholic ecumenism. But this would be contrary to fact. It would, moreover, contradict the most recent pontifical documents. It has been noticed, and rightly so, that these letters "present Catholic doctrine in a vocabulary and with an emphasis for which we have no parallel" [3] in the acts of the Sovereign Pontiffs since Leo XIII. Thus, since 1864 and 1865 the terms "heretics" and "schismatics" are not used to denote individuals in good faith. The vocabulary used since that time reserves those terms to persons who found heresies or start schisms, presuming that they wilfully revolt.[4] These expressions also refer to Churches or separated groups, in which case they simply designate a fact, without passing any judgment as to responsibilities. As for Christians today who are born into Orthodoxy, Anglicanism, or Protestantism, they are usually always referred to as *dissidentes,* separated. The use of their proper name is not excluded, for example *Orthodoxi,*[5] *Ecclesiae Orientales.*[6]

Pope Leo XIII is mainly responsible for this change in vocabulary. It evidently implies no modification of doctrine. Yet, it calls for a fresh examination of the problem of Christian reunion.

Leo XIII introduced prayer for Christian union that would

---

[2] Edward Hanahoe, *Two Early Documents on Reunion,* 1954, p. 5.

[3] Gregory Baum, *op. cit.,* p. 152.

[4] Canon 1325, par. 2.

[5] Benedict XV, *Orientis catholici, Acta Ap. Sed.,* 1918, p. 533.

[6] See Yves Congar, *Notes sur les mots 'confession,' 'Englise,' et 'Communion,'* in *Irenikon,* 1950, pp. 3-36.

not expect the immediate conversion of the Orthodox and the Protestants, but rather the rapprochement of the separated brethren. Stated in another way, Leo XIII saw prayer for unity in a truly ecumenical context.

The Sovereign Pontiff has not always been appreciated as the precursor that he was. In 1835 the Italian priest Vincent Pallotti (1795-1850), whom Pius XII beatified in 1950, had conceived the idea of consecrating the octave of the feast of the Epiphany to prayer for the universality of the faith. The Epiphany was Christ's first manifestation of Himself to the nations, who were represented by the magi of the Gospel. As we know, its commemoration is the most ancient form of the feast of Christmas. In the official liturgical calendar of the Church it enjoys even more solemnity than Christmas. Pallotti wanted to bring this to light. During the octave of the Epiphany he organized preaching and prayer sessions. These were dedicated to the theme of the universality of the faith and the unity of the Church. The use of different languages for preaching made this universality more tangible. Vincent Pallotti intended that this solemn celebration of the octave gradually restore the meaning of Epiphany. He hoped that the Epiphany would become a visible focus of Christian unity. But this practice did not spread beyond the Diocese of Rome itself.

The explicit purpose of this prayer was that the Church be granted unity. This is not necessarily ecumenical, but why should the Church pray for a unity which she already has, unless this unity ought to be more manifest? The best manifestation of unity may well be that Christians form but one flock in the eyes of unbelievers. In other words, any prayer for Church unity is implicitly ecumenical. It includes brotherhood and rapprochement among Christians.

Leo XIII was mindful of this. In his apostolic letter *Provida Matris* of May 5, 1895, he consecrated the nine days preceding Pentecost to prayer for Christian unity. On May 9, 1897 the encyclical *Divinum illud,* on the doctrine of the

Holy Spirit, restated this intention. Thus, prayer for Christian unity was related to devotion to the Holy Spirit. It was placed under the eminently inspiring sign of the Spirit. Individual conversions of separated Christians was not the officially designated purpose of this prayer. It had an organic rapprochement expressly in mind, "reconciliation to the faith of all those who are separated from the Church in questions of faith or jurisdiction." [7] It dealt with "the perfection of the gift of Christian unity." [8]

Likewise in 1883, when Leo XIII inaugurated prayers for the month of October, thereafter called the month of the rosary, he mentioned Church unity among his intentions. "That all those who have received baptism may be united in Christ and with each other by the bonds of one faith and perfect love." [9] That Mary "establish her world-wide family in a holy unity." [10]

The inclusion of the desire for a collective rapprochement of Christians in the prayer for Church unity is in keeping with Leo XIII's views on the meaning of separation. When the Orthodox quit the Roman Communion and the Protestants rejected a number of dogmas of faith, it located the separated Christians outside of Christianity. The Holy Father explicitly differentiated between missionary work and work for unity. According to the encyclical *Christi nomen* (December 24, 1894), the former consists in inviting "pagans, wherever they may be, to the unity of the Christian faith." The latter, on the contrary, "furthers return to the One Church." [11]

The encyclical *Grande munus* (September 30, 1880) also suggests that in a sense there is not yet one flock and one shepherd. Catholic unity is a fact. But it must serve as an example "to all those who adore Christ but who are sepa-

---

[7] *Divinum illud, Leonis XIII Allocutiones*, vol. 7, 1906, p. 20.
[8] *Ibid.*, p. 33.
[9] *Fidentem piumque*, September 20, 1896, *ibid.*, vol. 6, 1900, p. 217.
[10] *Adjutricem populi*, September 5, 1895, *ibid.*, vol. 6, 1900, p. 96.
[11] *Christi nomen, ibid.*, vol. 6, 1900, p. 8.

rated from the Roman Church, so that there may be but one flock and one shepherd." [12] Leo XIII remarked that "from time to time the course of human events gives some natural indications that lead us to hope that the peoples of the East, who have been separated from the bosom of the Church for a long time will, please God, be reconciled with her some day." [13] This will call for a work of long duration. We should not content ourselves with waiting. "Rather, we should meet them and open our arms to embrace them on their return." [14] Leo XIII did his best to hasten the reconciliation by "going out to meet" the separated Christians. He said that everything he did during his pontificate had but two purposes: to restore Christian life to society and the family, and to prepare for the reconciliation of Christians. [15]

In 1894 the Pope devoted the encyclical *Praeclara gratulationis* to the problem of unity. This was the first papal document dedicated to ecumenism. Leo XIII addressed himself to the Orthodox, and said, "We are looking for rapprochement and union not under the influence of some human motive, surely, but out of divine love and zeal for the common good." [16] Leo XIII felt that the less difference there is between East and West the easier it is to achieve a rapprochement. Speaking of the Orthodox Churches, he wrote that: "The line that separates us is not very wide. Moreover, apart from a few points, there is such a complete agreement on everything else that we oftentimes rely on the authorities and reasons for doctrines, customs and rites of the Eastern Churches for the defense of the Catholic faith." [17]

The Pope also launched an appeal to the Protestants for rapprochement. "All of you, whoever you may be, who for

---

[12] See Roger Aubert, *Le Saint-Siège et l'Union des Eglises*, p. 45, 1946.
[13] Aubert, *ibid.*, p. 44.
[14] Aubert, *ibid.*, p. 45.
[15] *Divinum illud, op. cit.*, p. 20.
[16] Aubert, *op. cit.*, p. 34.
[17] Aubert, *loc. cit.*, p. 34.

one reason or other are separated from us, let us rejoin in the unity of the faith and knowledge of the Son of God. Allow us to extend our hand to you with affection and to lead you to that unity which the Catholic Church has never lost, and which no one can take away from her. This common mother has been calling you to her bosom for a long time. For a long time Catholics all over the world have awaited you, with the anxiousness of brotherly love, that you might serve God with us in the unity of the same Gospel, the same faith, the same hope, bound by perfect love." [18] This is a call to Catholic unity. Yet, Leo XIII was not expecting numerous conversions. Rather, he was hoping for a gradual rapprochement. "Thus, the work that we have undertaken will be . . . a long and painful task, and its success is a considerably long way off." [19] These are long-term projects that aspire to collective rapprochements. Only these can recover the lost benefits of union. "If concord has been preserved, then a common participation having great and numerous benefits has been kept." [20] For this reason Leo XIII did not hesitate to address himself to groups and not just to individuals. His apostolic letter *Amantissimae voluntatis,* of April 14, 1895, was addressed *Ad Anglos,* "to the English who seek the kingdom of Christ in the unity of the faith."

Leo XIII was especially interested in the problems of Anglicanism. He personally followed the debates on the subject of Anglican ordinations. He talked with Abbé Portal and with Lord Halifax as well. His decision to have Anglican orders studied was made in response to the Anglo-Catholics' desire to remove an obstacle to reconciliation. As we know, the conclusion was negative. The encyclical *Apostolicae curae,* September 13, 1896, declared Anglican ordinations null and void. The Pope knew that this would shatter many

---

[18] Aubert, *op. cit.,* p. 36-7.

[19] *Optissimae,* March 19, 1895; see Aubert, *op. cit.,* p. 58.

[20] *Urbanitatis veteris,* November 20, 1901; see Aubert, *op. cit.,* p. 65.

hopes. Nevertheless he considered it no obstacle to continued preparation for reunion. In effect, he exhorted those charged with the care of souls in the Anglican Church to continue to have "the glory of God and the salvation of souls" at heart, in hope of a reconciliation. He was dreaming of a reunion that would serve as a model to "individuals and communities." [21]

Leo XIII addressed Anglicanism again in the aforementioned letter *Amantissimae voluntatis.* "God is witness to the lively hope that we entertain of seeing our efforts help promote and bring about this great work of obtaining Christian unity in England." [22] The Pope asked that everyone cooperate for this end. "With deep affection, we invite all of you in England, no matter what community or institution you belong to, to carry through with the holy purpose of returning to union." We may have to wait a long time for results, "but is that a reason for abandoning all hope of reconciliation and peace? Not at all." [23]

The encyclical *Caritatis studium* (July 25, 1898) dealt with unity inasmuch as it was especially concerned with Protestantism. This letter was addressed to the Episcopate of Scotland. It studied the religious problems of Scotland. But the keynote of it is the problem of Protestantism, since the majority of Scots belong to the Presbyterian Church. The Pope again expressed his anxiety for unity. "Each day we regret more and more the unhappy state of so many people who lack the Christian faith in its entirety." All his efforts are to the end that "they may one day be willing to join us in restoring the communion of one and the same faith. This is a big project, and it is almost impossible to realize through human means. It belongs to God alone, to whom everything is possible, to bring it about. That is why we will not give up hope, and the abundance of difficulties that human power

---

[21] *Apostolicae curae, op. cit.,* vol. 6, p. 209.
[22] Aubert, *op. cit.,* p. 72.
[23] Aubert, *op. cit.,* p. 76.

cannot avert of itself does not turn us aside from this project." [24] After speaking of the history of Catholic Scotland, Leo XIII laid the foundations for a dialogue with Protestantism. Scripture, which the Protestants received from the Church, remains common to both Confessions. It constitutes a bond of unity. "The Scots deserve the highest congratulations for being assiduous in their study of and love for Sacred Scripture. This high regard for the study of Sacred Scripture is a kind of relationship with the Catholic Church, so to speak. Couldn't this be the beginning of the unity that is to be regained? Let them not pretend to have forgotten that it is the Catholic Church and none other from whom they have received the Books of the Two Testaments." [25] Scripture is not completely self-explanatory. Differences in interpretation are ample evidence for the necessity of union and peace in unity.

A second point in common has already been mentioned, namely, the love of Christ. "Many Scots, while differing from us in faith, love the name of Christ with their whole soul and try to follow His doctrine and imitate His holy examples." [26] This amounts to being a Catholic leaven, because whoever knows Christ wants to know and share in the fulness of Christianity. The Pope ends his letter with an appeal that all Catholics help in the work of unity.

Pope Leo XIII hereby once again proposed the bases for a Catholic ecumenism. Initially it consists in seeking points of contact between Protestants and Catholics, such as Scripture and love for Christ. Starting out from here, it will bring to light the fulness of tradition, which is implied in Scripture itself, and the fulness of revelation, implied in the love of Christ. Hence there is no true Catholic ecumenism without a return to the sources.

Father Gregory Baum summarizes the concept of ecu-

---

24 *Leonis XIII Allocutiones*, vol. 7, p. 150.
25 *Ibid.*, p. 153.
26 *Ibid.*, p. 155.

menism deduced from the papal documents beginning with
Leo XIII by saying that Catholic ecumenism is "the Church's
appointed function in severed Christianity which consists in
fostering towards perfection the wounded Christian patri-
monies in dissidence and in reducing towards elimination the
human falsifications associated with them." [27] Leo XIII was
the first Pope to take up ecumenism. He must be given credit
for laying the bases of modern Catholic ecumenism. It will
be possible for Benedict XV, Pius XI and Pius XII to
elaborate a highly developed ecumenical position on this
foundation. The main point was already made by Leo XIII.

---

[27] Gregory Baum, *op. cit.*, p. 97-8.

PART two

THE

TWENTIETH

CENTURY

CHAPTER VIII

NINETEEN-TEN

"Just because Unity is the greatest and deepest of our needs, just because its restoration would be so great a sign and result of God's favour to a penitent and purified Church, we are unable and unworthy yet to speak about it in any practical way. It can only come by penitence: all penitence is hard, and corporate penitence, to judge from history, is the hardest of all."
—E. S. Talbot, Anglican Bishop of Southwark

The World Missionary Conference of Edinburgh inaugurated twentieth century ecumenism in 1910. In a sense it was only a step, but the most fruitful one, in the development of missionary conferences. It was the first of such conferences that might be designated as universal in fact and ecumenical in spirit. Still, it was not absolutely universal. The Catholic missions, and there were many of them, were neither represented nor invited. The Orthodox Churches, which have a few missionaries, were absent. There was a very unequal representation of the Protestant world. The Anglo-Saxon element dominated the Assembly. An attempt was made, however, to admit to the conference Anglican societies that

95

followed the "High Church" theology. Up to now these societies had boycotted the missionary conferences. They rightly suspected the Protestant mind of their organizers. They felt that they would have to keep silent about their catholic interpretation of Anglicanism and of missionary work. Consequently the Anglican Communion was represented at the interconfessional missionary meetings only by societies having a "Low Church," that is to say, a Protestant theology. The program of the Edinburgh Conference changed this state of affairs by assuaging the Anglo-Catholics' fears. Encouraged by a number of Anglican prelates, the *Society for the Propagation of the Gospel* sent a large delegation to Edinburgh.

It was understood beforehand that the Conference would not discuss doctrine but action. It seemed that this negative basis was necessary for an initial meeting between Anglo-Catholic and Protestant delegates. Not everybody was satisfied with this arrangement. Some of the delegates wanted to go further. The American Anglican delegation was able to take the initiative in this respect.

American Anglicanism had profited by an outstanding ecumenical tradition even before going to Edinburgh. Very little influenced by the Oxford Movement, it formulated the ecumenical vocation of Anglicanism in very curious terms during the nineteenth century. In 1841 Thomas Hubbard Vail (1812-89) had proposed that all American Protestants join together in the Episcopal Church, which was the one most capable of assuring a true Christian unity.[1] In 1853 William August Muhlenberg (1786-1877) suggested that the Episcopal Church modify its constitution. He felt that American Protestants desiring to join the Anglican Communion should be able to do so without adopting all its practices or all of its doctrine. His overall plan was to have two concentric Churches. The Episcopal Church would be the nucleus. Another Church, less constrained by the Anglican tradition,

---

[1] *The Comprehensive Church, or, Christian unity and ecclesiastical union in the Protestant Episcopal Church,* Hartford, 1841.

would radiate around this.[2] Finally, in 1870, William Reed
Huntington (1838-1918) again invited American Protestantism to join the Church of reconciliation, the Episcopal Church.
His four conditions for entering it became well known as the
Lambeth Quadrilateral. In 1898 Huntington formulated
another project. It had to do with a detailed plan of union
that would result in a National American Church along the
Anglican plan, but which would incorporate many features
of all known forms of Church government.[3]

The American Anglican tradition encountered other ecumenical traditions at Edinburgh. There was the missionary
tradition, which had no patience with Christian divisions.
There were also the Christian youth movements. In order
to win the Anglo-Catholics they had adopted the discussion
methods of the Young Men's Christian Association, with
whom the Anglo-Catholics had already been working. Joseph
Oldham, the secretary of the Edinburgh Conference, had
already been secretary of the British Christian Students'
Movement. The president, John Mott (1865-1955), was
one of the founders of the International Federation of Christian Students.

The missionary movement, the student movements, and
American Anglicanism converged on Edinburgh. All three
had an impassioned interest in Christian unity. The participants in the Edinburgh Conference were characterized by
a living though not defined unity. Doctrinal differences between Churches were not discussed. They simply dealt with
missionary problems. There was nevertheless an atmosphere
of unity, as many of the speakers noted. Moreover, there
was a Commission on Co-operation and the Promotion of
Unity.

The most significant accomplishment on the organizational

_____

[2] *Evangelical Catholic Papers,* ed. by Anne Ayes, 2 v., New York,
1875.

[3] *The Church Idea: An Essay Toward Unity,* 1870; *A National
Church,* 1898.

level was the creation of a permanent committee. In 1921 this resulted in the formation of the International Missionary Council, which would later maintain increasingly close relations with the World Council of Churches.

In the sphere of ideas, the thing that was new about Edinburgh was that it took up a suggestion brought up at the end of the Conference by an American Anglican bishop, Charles Brent (1862-1929), a missionary in the Philippine Islands. "During these past days," he said, "a new vision has been unfolded to us. But when God gives a vision He also points to some new responsibility. And you and I, when we leave this assembly, we will go away with new duties to perform." [4] The vision Brent saw was that of a single Church. The new duty he felt himself charged with was that of organizing an interconfessional reunion to deal with what was excluded at Edinburgh, namely, the doctrinal differences of Christians. Somewhat later, on October 19, 1910, the General Convention of the Episcopal Church of the United States appointed a commission to bring about "a conference for the consideration of questions touching on the faith and order of the Church." It vowed that "all Christian Communions throughout the world which confess our Lord Jesus Christ as God and Saviour would be asked to unite with us in arranging for and conducting such a conference."

The "Faith and Order" movement was born.

"Faith and Order" is foremost an organization that prepares studies on comparative doctrine. It is concerned with "studying the issues on which we differ, in the hope that a better understanding of different points of view in regard to the faith and order of the Church will incite a deeper desire for unity." [5] We will not stop to examine the various difficulties that postponed the date of the first conference that was planned. Many were not convinced of the feasibility of such

---

[4] Quoted in Ruth Rouse-Stephen Neill, *op. cit.,* p. 407.
[5] Rouse-Neill, *ibid.,* p. 408.

a project. The German Lutherans, who somewhat distrusted Anglicans, stayed away for a long time. While Pope Benedict XV heartily encouraged the organizers, he courteously declined their invitation. The work of preparation ceased during the War of 1914. The Churches justified the politics of their governments on a doctrinal basis, which made a purely doctrinal discussion impossible. The German Churches after the war persisted in remaining aloof. A commission got together in Geneva in 1920 to decide what topics the General Assembly would take up. The Conference of Lausanne was finally convoked on August 3, 1927.

It has often been said that the very idea of "Faith and Order" is Anglican.[6] There were Lutherans at Lausanne beyond the shade of a doubt. The German Churches had finally sent delegates. There were also Calvinists and Orthodox present. They all took part in the discussions and divided up the presidencies and secretaryships. Still, the program was more in accord with the Anglican turn of mind rather than with the Lutheran or the Calvinist. It included the following sections: [7]

(1) The call to unity.
(2) The Church's message to the world: the Gospel.
(3) The nature of the Church.
(4) The Church's confession of faith.
(5) The ministry of the Church.
(6) The sacraments.
(7) Christian unity and the position of the various Churches.

After a discussion on the texts prepared by the committee, a statement on each of these themes was voted on. Once adopted, this statement had to be passed on to the Churches

---

[6] Information on this subject may be found in Yves Congar, *Chrétiens Désunis*, and Gustave Thils, *Histoire Doctrinale du Mouvement Oecuménique*.

[7] *Faith and Order. Proceedings of the World Conference*, 1927.

for whom it was being studied. But the Orthodox delegates would have no part with any of the statements except the second. And as the result of a Lutheran motion, no vote took place on the seventh report.

Anglican doctrine is essentially an ecclesiology, and this was the general theme of the Lausanne Assembly. The fundamental theme of Lutheranism, justification, was not even mentioned. Evidently all of the traditions could express their opinion on each statement, and the fourth, which was on the confession of faith, provoked a bitter dispute. The general orientation of the themes however, was centered around the Anglican and Catholic idea of the historic nature of the Church. It further suggested a kind of unity between Churches that was not well defined, something that Anglicanism had been interested in for a long time. To those who were influenced by sources other than Anglicanism "unity among Churches" meant about the same thing as "unity of the Church." The organizers of the Conference had to muster all their patience to keep repeating day after day that it was not a question of creating one united Church but only of seeking out the ways of the Lord by means of doctrinal inquiries. The Anglicans believed in the unity and historical continuity of the Church. They knew that unity ultimately is unity in the faith. They repeatedly had to prevent the discussion from turning into a study of practical ways to achieve unity. On the whole, this Anglican orientation remained one of agreements that were brought up and adopted.

From this point of view the Lausanne Conference was the answer to the appeal made by Bishop Brent in 1910. It initiated Protestantism to a study of the unity given to the Church. This made it possible to hope for an end to Christian divisions.

Lausanne put Protestants having a Lutheran or Calvinist background into contact with Anglican thought. The Anglicanism in question was not exactly the Anglo-Catholicism that derived from the Oxford Movement and which was close to Catholicism. It was a "Low Church" Anglicanism, but anchored in the Anglican historic tradition more than that of the continental Reformation. It had, moreover, mixed in with this a certain number of "High Church" ideas. Thanks to a number of work committees, these contacts and exchanges of thought were kept up after the Conference. These committees prepared a second assembly which opened at Edinburgh on August 3, 1937.[8]

This time again delegates came from all or almost all parts of the world. The Germans couldn't come to Edinburgh because Adolf Hitler's government refused them passports. The Orthodox delegates, faithful to their patristic heritage, again voiced their opposition to the theology of the proposed statements.

These statements dealt with the general theme of the Church, as before. But the increasing importance of non-Anglican theologies was evidenced by the subjects studied. The five sections of the theme of the Assembly come under the following headings:

(1) The grace of our Lord Jesus Christ.
(2) The Church of Christ and the Word of God.
(3) The Church of Christ: ministry and sacraments.
(4) The unity of the Church in life and worship.
(5) The communion of saints.

This time the subject of grace opens the discussion. The Church is also seen in a double relationship to the Word and to the Sacraments. The idea of grace is more central to Lutheranism than to Anglicanism. The definition of the Church in terms of the Word and the Sacraments is common to both Lutheranism and Calvinism. If it had a place in the Thirty-nine Articles of the Church of England in the sixteenth century, it did not maintain the central place in subsequent Anglican thought. From the Protestant viewpoint, then, the

---

[8] *The Second World Conference on Faith and Order,* 1938.

Edinburgh discussions were more balanced than those of Lausanne. This was partly due to the fact that the delegates felt more at ease the second time they met. But it was also because of the subjects studied. The history of "Faith and Order" uncovered the syndromes of a phenomenon that has continued to manifest itself: a progressive replacement of Anglicanism by Lutheran and Calvinist Protestantism in the direction of the "Faith and Order" movement.

The Edinburgh Assembly was the last plenary meeting of "Faith and Order" as a distinct movement. With the formation of the World Council of Churches, which was settled on shortly after the Edinburgh Assembly, "Faith and Order" was incorporated into the Council. It kept a relatively distinct existence as the commission in charge of studying doctrinal questions arising from the ecumenical movement. "Faith and Order" continued its customary interconfessional conferences. From now on they were held within the framework of the World Council of Churches. Thus the Lund Conference [9] held in 1952 can be studied in line with those of Lausanne and Edinburgh.

The Lund Conference took up three subjects:

(1) The nature of the Church.
(2) Ways of worship.
(3) Intercommunion.

A volume was prepared on each of these subjects before the Conference. It would have been desirable that the delegates read these books before going to Lund, but not all of them did so. Nevertheless, a fruitful dialogue ensued. The best of the German Lutheran tradition, demanding a change of method and mainly represented by Edmond Schlink, a professor at Heidelberg, dominated the debates. Up to this time "Faith and Order" contented itself with comparing doctrines. But no one can be indefinitely satisfied with making

---

[9] *The Third World Conference on Faith and Order,* 1953.

comparisons. One must go a step further and pass judgment on doctrine with the help of a more extensive study of the New Testament and a deeper understanding of tradition.

Therefore Lund made a step forward: the development of doctrinal self-criticism. This introduced a new element into the ecumenical dialogue, namely, the study of tradition and its rightful place in the Church. In fact, two commissions were established after the Lund Conference, one in Europe and another in America, for the purpose of studying the concept of tradition. This was indicative that tremendous progress had been made since the Edinburgh Conference. Tradition would henceforth be associated with the Word, on which the Edinburgh Assembly had centered its emphasis. The Orthodox, who were always present at the "Faith and Order" conferences in spite of the serious misgivings they had about some of the tendencies of the movement, may be given credit for exercising some influence here. The mark made by Anglicanism, which has always associated Church tradition with Holy Scripture, must also be recognized. And German and Swiss Lutheran theology contributed to bringing up this fundamental problem.

Lund also opened up a new topic, the liturgy. This permitted a convergence of ecumenism with the liturgical movements that were at work among the Anglican and Lutheran and even the Calvinist Churches. By studying worship and intercommunion it made the ecumenical world aware of contemporary liturgical revivals. This again represented considerable progress. Faith and the tradition of the Church express themselves by worship. To return to the liturgy means to restore the consciousness of communal action and, as a result, consciousness of the Church as an institution.

We must not deceive ourselves by presuming that conclusions favourable to Catholicism will easily be reached. But nothing should surprise us. Changes of thought that produce results always come about slowly. Structural changes in theological thought require extensive preparations. Ecumenism must be given time to develop its theological depths.

With Lund we may close this brief study of the movement that was born in 1910. Since 1952 regional conferences of "Faith and Order" have been held, notably at Oberlin in the United States in 1957. Though they are of some importance, these do not carry the weight of world conferences. The studies undertaken by "Faith and Order" have made progress, especially in regard to tradition and its place in the Church. But we must still wait patiently for these studies to make an impact on the Churches themselves.

We have mentioned the gradual replacement of Anglicanism by other theologies in "Faith in Order." This is constantly felt. But Anglicanism is there, and it has not lost its role as catalyst. Other traditions have taken up doctrinal problems first raised by Anglicans. Nothing can make us forget that "Faith and Order" is due to the initiative of Charles Brent, a missionary bishop of the Episcopal Church of the United States.

CHAPTER IX

LIFE AND WORK

"Doctrine divides; service unites."

The first concern of Catholics is doctrine. In this respect they differ from most Protestants. The method of doctrinal comparison adopted by the "Faith and Order" movement was not designed to please all the Reformation Christians. Thus, between 1910 and 1940 there were two ecumenical movements. The first, "Faith and Order," made doctrinal discussion the order of the day. The second, "Practical Christianity," also called "Life and Work," disregarded doctrinal discussion. Consequently, ecumenism developed along two distinct patterns.

But if they were distinct, there was no complete division between the two. Most of the people who were active in one movement were active in the other, so there was no opposition and rivalry between them. There were just differences in viewpoints and immediate purpose. Organizations that see Christian unity as their ultimate goal can certainly have in mind different steps towards achieving that unity. They can

105

therefore settle on temporal accomplishments and interme-diate goals that differ.

The viewpoint of "Life and Work" was eminently prac-tical. It was concerned with working together on projects which required no preliminary dogmatic discussions. But many questions urgently demanded a Christian answer. In 1914 it was the problem of the war and peace. What is the Christian judgment on war? Must the Churches campaign for the cessation of hostilities? Under what conditions should peace be asked for or granted? Should political action be taken in undertaking such an effort for the sake of peace? To what extent can the Church mix in politics? Connected problems were raised after the war. Are the Churches obliged to condemn those who are responsible for the war? Who is responsible? Should the German Churches confess their fault or at the very least admit their negligence? On the other hand, should they refuse to take the blame?

Once the after-effects of the First World War began to sub-side, an economic crisis broke out in a lot of countries. The Churches were again faced with practical problems regarding the economic organization of society. Should they condemn the laissez-faire policy of capitalism, which is responsible for the economic chaos? What stand should be taken on social rights? Does the worker movement contain a latent Chris-tianity? What should they think of Bolshevism?

Finally, national socialism drew their attention. German Lutheranism found itself divided into two camps. The self-styled "German Christians" favored Nazism. The "Confes-sional Church" was hostile to the regime and was persecuted. Should the other Churches choose sides? Was it possible to decide which one of the camps was the sole representative of a true Christianity? Many questions were raised by stresses and strains between Church and State. The Confessional Church condemned the Nazi State. But Lutheranism, tradi-tionally unconcerned with political problems, had always respected the divine right of the royal state. Was there then another Christian concept of Church-State relations? Should the separation of the religious and the civil, as upheld by modern Calvinism, contrary to the Calvinism of old, become a norm for the Churches?

These were at first practical questions, but they gradually became theoretical. How could relations between Church and State be argued without touching on the nature of the Church? Besides, as soon as you consult the Bible as a rule of thumb, you are involved in Scripture study and by that very fact, in doctrine. In fact, "Life and Work" was to bring up decidedly doctrinal questions. This was not so when the movement began.

"Life and Work" owes its origin to Nathan Söderblom (1866-1931), Lutheran Bishop of Upsala. French Protestants are pleased to know that a number of great French Protestants blazed the trail.[1] Tommy Fallot, Wilfred Monot, Elie Gounelle and others proposed ideas that were similar to those of Söderblom. It was his patience and tenacity in refusing to be discouraged that brought about the realization of actual collaboration on an international level.

The situation created by the First World War was, as a matter of fact, favorable to such an effort. "Faith and Order" stopped all activity during the War. Söderblom himself belonged to the modern Swedish tradition. He saw peace as the supreme good of nations, so he tried to get the Churches, even those in belligerent nations, to sign statements in favor of peace. He wasn't very successful. Neither the Germans, nor the Anglo-Saxons or the French were in a mood to concede one iota to their enemy. Just the same, Söderblom gained worldwide notoriety through his appeal for peace in November, 1917. In December, 1917, he succeeded in organizing a conference at Upsala. He did not get the Churches of the countries that were at war to participate, despite his desires. Only a few Germans ventured to come, as individ-

---

[1] See Paul Conord, *op. cit.,* pp. 53-63.

uals. It is typical of Söderblom's preoccupations that the Upsala Conference treated three principal problems: (1) Christian unity; (2) Christians and society; (3) Christians and international law.

Once the War ended, Söderblom wanted to reconcile the Churches of enemy countries with one another. This was no easy matter. A conference called at Oud Wassenaar in Holland from September 30 to October 3, 1919, was boycotted by the French Reformed Churches. Before agreeing to meet with the German Churches the French demanded an official declaration from them blaming Germany for her war acts.

As soon as he was able, Söderblom took up a project that he had thought about for a long time. He would settle for nothing less than establishing an international council of Churches. The purpose of such an organization would be to show Christian unity to the world by means of common acts. This is when the movement that was to result in the "Faith and Order" conferences came to life. Söderblom personally played a leading role in it. One might therefore wonder why the two movements did not develop as one. For Söderblom, as for a good part of Protestantism in his day, life was more important than doctrine. But the Anglicans who organized "Faith and Order" chose a path to unity which would involve doctrinal discussions. Söderblom felt that there was another way, namely that of action.

"Life and Work" reached the point of holding its first world conference more quickly than "Faith and Order." It was faced with fewer obstacles and objections than a conference centering around doctrinal unity. The first world conference that was properly speaking ecumenical was held at Stockholm from August 19-29, 1925.

The preparation had been long and intense.[2] Yet, one could hardly help being amazed at the adventurous and even chaotic character of the assemblies of "Life and Work."

---

[2] G.K.A. Bell (ed.): *The Stockholm Conference*, 1926.

Those of "Faith and Order" were less disputatious, even though dealing with more controversial questions. Six topics had been prepared for Stockholm to agree upon:

(1) The Church's duty in the light of God's plan for the world.
(2) The Church and economic and industrial problems.
(3) The Church and social and moral problems.
(4) The Church and international relations.
(5) The Church and education.
(6) Cooperation between Churches.

The scope of this program is impressive. It was the more difficult to treat since one point was to remain constantly ill-defined, namely, the Church, always the center of discussion yet never defined. The Conference, moreover, did not get much involved. After laborious discussions it contented itself with addressing a message to the Churches that is interesting and moving but which says little on the whole. Even in the field of economic and social questions the only thing original about Stockholm was the international character of the Conference. Stockholm was already left behind in the field of ideas. The Christians of Great Britain had held a conference on political, economic, and civic problems in Birmingham in April, 1924. Everything said at Stockholm had already been recorded in the twelve volumes of this Conference, styled COPEC. Besides, COPEC's statements were more ecumenical than those of the Stockholm discussions. The English Roman Catholics had actively participated in the Conference.

A doctrinal issue is nevertheless to be retained from the Stockholm Conference. Two Protestant tendencies showed up there. The first, which was particularly predominant in German Lutheranism, conceived the kingdom of God on a purely religious and theological level. It attempted to illustrate its transcendence by analogy with the kingdoms of this world. The second prevailed in Anglo-Saxon Protestantism and even deeply affected French Protestantism. It insisted on building the kingdom of God on earth. Sometimes it would even see purely temporal institutions like the League of Nations as instruments of the kingdom of God. These two tendencies are still encountered in ecumenical Protestantism.

In spite of its drawbacks, the Stockholm Conference constituted an important step in the advance of ecumenism. For the first time, Protestants from all over the world met with Orthodox prelates face to face. Stockholm might be reproached for the weak participation of Churches from mission countries, nowadays referred to as the "younger Churches." We might also regret the weakness of the Orthodox, almost drowned in a Protestant sea, and the excessive importance given Anglo-Saxon Protestantism. All of this is true, but it simply means that the Stockholm Assembly was still not an ideal ecumenical assembly. It is not to be evaluated in terms of what took place at Stockholm itself, but in terms of the progressive rapprochement that it encouraged among Christians.

Söderblom was not confident at his success. The Stockholm Conference had been a personal triumph for him. He did not stop with that. A "Permanent Committee of Practical Christianity" was instituted. It set up a multitude of commissions which tried to follow up on the rapprochement already on the way. An International Christian Social Institute was established. The gifted Söderblom anticipated numerous aspects of the future World Council of Churches and of the Ecumenical Institute of Bossey. In 1930 a permanent committee even took the prophetic title of the "World Council" of Life and Work.

Some studies were published. They gave more and more importance to doctrinal questions on the nature of the Church, especially in its relations with the State. The struggle that German Christianity was having with national socialism made these studies necessary.[3]

---

[3] These titles are still useful: *Eglise, Foi et Ethique Sociale* (1934), *L'Eglise et le Problème de l'Etat aujourd'hui* (1935).

"Life and Work" was getting ready for its second world conference, which took place at Oxford, July 12-26, 1937. Here again we see the fruitful chaos that characterized the activities of Practical Christianity. An impressive series of local conferences had been held in preparation for the international meeting. Some books were published, for example *The Totalitarian State and Christian Freedom* (1937) and an extensive work written by Russian Orthodox theologians, *The Church, the State, and Man* (1937). The Conference was divided into five sections, each of which was assigned a topic:

(1) The Church and society.
(2) The Church and the State.
(3) The Church, society, and the State.
(4) The Church, society, and the State in relation to education.
(5) The universal Church and the nations of the world.

A report had been prepared on each of these topics. The Oxford delegates supplied a considerable amount of work. The statements were judged inadequate from the start. They had to be rewritten, and this took two weeks of intensive discussions.

Seen in the context of the entire ecumenical movement, the Oxford Assembly shows that it is impossible to separate doctrine from Christian practice. Resistance to the totalitarian State, which was the general topic, requires doctrinal justification. It took time for "Life and Work" to become aware of this fact. The ideas of social Christianity were too widespread in America as well as in Europe for the delegates to be very easily convinced. Some complained bitterly about the return to doctrine. But Protestantism as a whole was passing through a doctrinal phase. Karl Barth's influence had spread since 1919. The social gospel became once more the Gospel of the historic redemption of the Son of God made man. The Oxford delegates were also aware of the need for doctrine.

The Second "Faith and Order" Conference was to be held at Edinburgh from August 3-18, just a few days after the close of the Oxford Conference. The Oxford delegates proposed uniting the two movements.

The union of "Life and Work" and the "Faith and Order" movement gave birth to the World Council of Churches at Amsterdam in 1948. "Faith and Order" remained a commission of the Council, entrusted with doctrinal questions. "Life and Work" disappeared, but it did not actually cease existing. Its life simply passed on to a new organism that was heir to its multiple initiatives, rather blundering, but full of fervor. Söderblom himself had dreamed of an Ecumenical Council of Churches. But he had died in 1931, on this side of the Jordan, before the passage over into the promised land that he had caught sight of.

Charles Brent should be given the credit for initiating debates in view of doctrinal rapprochements. But Söderblom must be credited with the vision that gave rise to the World Council, which is the most important contribution of "Life and Work" to modern ecumenism.

CHAPTER X

FROM SAINT PIUS X TO PIUS XI

"For reunion, it is first of all necessary to know one another and to love one another."

—Pius XI

The time of the two parallel movements "Faith and Order" and "Practical Christianity" was a period of formation for ecumenism. This was true of Catholic ecumenism as well. It was more conscious of itself, more sure of its method, better established on a solid theological foundation at the close of this period than at its start. The era of Leo XIII had laid the foundations of Catholic ecumenical thought. Perhaps this beginning stage might be summarized as Leo XIII himself summarized it in speaking of the Orthodox Churches when he said: "Our eyes will never see the union of Churches that we are working for, but let us not be so faint-hearted as to regard this unceasing effort as a fanciful dream. Such a sentiment would be unworthy of a Christian." [1]

Twentieth century Catholicism started out from here, and

---

[1] Discourse given March 9, 1895; see Aubert, *op. cit.,* p. 57-8.

it was not easy going. The modernist era began about this time and it was not favorable to ecumenical activities. A calm ecumenism could hardly develop in a disturbed atmosphere. It is a good thing, moreover, that no one tried to confuse modernism with Christian rapprochement. Just the same, things turned out so that the work of union undertaken by Leo XIII progressed during the pontificate of Pius X. The Pontiff was engrossed with the very pressing question of defending the faith against the modernist heresy. It should not be forgotten that the final Christian reunion will only take place in the true faith. The spread of a new heresy, or, as the encyclical *Pascendi* called modernism, of a "synthesis of all heresies" must be seen as a contribution to the cause of a true ecumenical movement. By preserving true tradition, this movement makes true union possible. Anyhow, by his courageous struggle against modernism, Pius X succeeded in preventing a new schism. There is danger of one every time that such a widespread crisis shakes the Church. Pius X had better success than Leo X had when the latter was faced with growing Lutheranism. There was no new cleavage apart from the departure of a few individuals.

In Protestant ecumenism the year 1910 was the most significant in this entire era. No Catholic was present at the Missionary Conference of Edinburgh, but a long message from an Italian Catholic bishop was read there by one of the American participants, Silas McBee. Bishop Bonomelli of Cremona wrote a long letter of encouragement to the members of the Edinburgh Assembly. This letter deserves recognition. According to Bishop Bonomelli, the Edinburgh Conference gives evidence of a consoling fact:

"The most desirable and precious of human liberties, religious liberty, may now be said to be a grand conquest of contemporary humanity, and it enables men of various faiths to meet together, not for the purpose of hating and combating each other, for the supposed greater glory of God, but in order to consecrate themselves in Christian love to the pursuit of that religious truth which unites all believers in Christ. United in one faith, the various spiritual forces combine in the adoration of the one true God in spirit and in truth." [2]

The bishop then said that the Christians gathered together at Edinburgh were sufficiently united so as to be capable of working together:

"The elements of fact in which you all agree are numerous and are common to the various Christian denominations, and they can therefore serve as a point of departure for your discussions. It is, therefore, legitimate to aspire to a unity of faith and of religious practice, and to work for its realization by the consecration of all energies of mind and heart. This is a work in which we in our day may well cooperate." [3]

The letter listed some basic points common to all Christians: belief in God the Creator, belief in Christ the Redeemer, and the figure of Christ as God Incarnate.

"Thus we are united in the profound conviction that a universal religion is necessary, and that this must be the Christian religion; not a cold and formal religion, a thing apart from human life, but a living force, pervading the human soul in its essence, and its various manifestations—a religion, in short, which completes and crowns our life and which bears fruition in works of love and holiness." [4]

Finally, "the need of a Church which may be the outward manifestation of your faith and religious feeling, the vigilant custodian now and here of Christian doctrine and tradition" unites all believers.[5] Thus, "from the various Churches and religious denominations into which you Christians are divided there arises a new unifying element, a noble aspiration, re-

---

2 *World Missionary Conference,* 1910, vol. 8, p. 221.
3 *Ibid.,* p. 221.
4 *Ibid.,* p. 222.
5 *Ibid.,* p. 222.

straining too great impulsiveness, levelling off dividing barriers, and working for the realization of the one Holy Church through all the children of redemption." [6]

Bishop Bonomelli's letter is further evidence that some Catholic bishops were aware of the religious content of Protestant ecumenism before more recent times.

Towards the end of the pontificate of Pius X a correspondence was started between Robert Gardiner, one of the organizers of "Faith and Order," and the cardinal secretary of state, who at that time was Cardinal Gasparri. This exchange of letters continued under Benedict XV. At the time of the controversy over Anglican ordinations, Cardinal Gasparri, who was teaching canon law at the Catholic Institute in Paris, was sufficiently interested in the question to write some articles on it. Later, as secretary of state under Pius XI, Cardinal Gasparri expressed his sympathy with the Malines Conversations. He had therefore been won over to the cause of Christian unity and the apostolate for unity. The cardinal expressed Pope Benedict XV's hopes for the Malines Conversations. The purpose of the efforts made by the Sovereign Pontiffs is that "the one and only Church which Jesus Christ has decreed and sanctified by His divine blood be always carefully guarded and kept entire, unsullied, and ever overflowing with love." [7] The Holy Father hoped that, "struck by its natural beauty, and all quarrels being finished, you will be able to work successfully to the end that the Mystical Body of Christ will cease being broken and scattered, and that on the other hand unity of faith and communion might finally triumph among all humanity through harmony, spiritual cooperation, and concord." [8]

Pope Benedict XV therefore understood the problem facing "Faith and Order." Furthermore, he was greatly in-

---

[6] *Ibid.*, p. 222.

[7] Letter of December 18, 1914, quoted by Max Pribilla in *Um kirchlische Einheit*, p. 315.

[8] *Ibid.*, p. 315.

terested in other ways in the cause of Christian unity. He favored the Eastern Rites in the Church by creating the Congregation for the Oriental Churches, and by founding the Pontifical Institute of Oriental Studies. The purpose of these moves was undoubtedly to strengthen the position of the Eastern Churches that were in communion with Rome. But in the Pope's mind these institutions were also to be centres of contact with Eastern Orthodoxy. The *motu proprio, Orientis catholici,* of October 15, 1917, by which the Oriental Institute was erected, even used the expression *Orthodoxi,* which was a term rarely employed in pontifical documents.

It was most unfortunate that Benedict XV, despite his interest in the unity movements and the encouragements that he had lavished on them, was obliged to turn down the invitation given to the Catholic Church to participate in the great assemblies that were pending. On June 19, 1918, the cardinal secretary of state advised the primates of Sweden, Norway, and Denmark that the Catholic Church would not participate in the international conference to which they had invited her. On July 4, 1919, a decree of the Holy Office forbade taking part in congresses that separated Christians held with a view to Christian unity, unless by express permission of the Holy See. On May 16, 1919, the Holy Father received the deputation that came to invite him to a "Faith and Order" conference. The official response handed to the visitors said that: "The teaching and practice of the Roman Catholic Church regarding the unity of the visible Church of Christ is well known to everybody, and therefore it would not be possible for the Catholic Church to take part in a congress such as the one proposed. His Holiness, however, by no means wishes to disapprove of the congress in question for those who are not in union with the chair of Peter." [9] Again, in April, 1921, Cardinal Gasparri wrote to the primates of

---

[9] Quoted in Rouse-Neill, *op. cit.,* p. 416.

the Scandinavian countries to thank them for the invitation
extended the Pope to participate in an assembly of "Practical Christianity." This letter, addressed to some Lutheran
prelates, like that of June, 1918, honored them with the rather
flattering title of *perillustres viri,* "most illustrious men." This
little expression of politeness was taken by the Protestant
world as a concealed insult. How carefully we should watch
the least details of our relations with our separated brethren!

The pontificate of Benedict XV seems to have acted as a
realistic reminder. It would be unbecoming for the Sovereign
Pontiff to participate in ecumenical conferences if he were to
join Protestants in trying to find out what kind of unity Christ
intended His Church to have. To the extent that this was
intended by inviting Benedict XV, the Holy Father could not
help but answer as he did. The Protestant world is under an
illusion if it imagines that the Catholic Church can change
her doctrine on unity. Such a change would not conform to
the truth, and there can be no rapprochement except in truth.

The biographers of Pius XI, Benedict XV's successor,
have often pointed out that he was deeply interested in unity
movements. His activity in favor of the apostolate for unity
had two characteristics. First, Pius XI interested himself in
Eastern Orthodoxy more than in Protestantism. Second, being a scholar himself, he had an intellectual apostolate
primarily in mind.

In 1922 Pius XI reorganized the Oriental Institute and
strongly encouraged the study of Oriental theology. At his
instigation the Catholic faculties of theology began introducing courses in Eastern theology into their program of studies.
In the encyclical *Rerum orientalium,* of September 8, 1929,
the Holy Father ordered the introduction of similar courses
in all major seminaries. On March 21, 1924, Pius XI addressed the Abbot Primate of the Order of Saint Benedict,
the Most Rev. Fidelius von Stötzingen, asking him to in-
augurate Oriental studies in the Benedictine Order. The
Pope's idea was to have some monks specialize in the study

of Eastern theology and liturgy, and to get them together in monasteries that would become centres of action in the unity apostolate. In a word, he wanted to establish Benedictine monasteries of the Byzantine Rite.

The first monastery entirely devoted to the cause of union was founded at Amay in Belgium in 1925. In 1929 it was transferred to Chevetogne, where it still flourishes. It is worth noting that in the letter *Equidem verba,* addressed to Dom von Stötzingen, Pius XI used an expression that was favored at the time. He spoke of "the work of the unionistic restoration." The purpose of this work as Pius XI described it, is that "all nations, freed from all discord, return to the unity of the Catholic Church, and that finally there might be but one flock and one shepherd." [10] His method would be to "pray unceasingly for unity and to undertake works towards this end." [11] The main work mentioned is study of the "languages, history, customs, character, and above all, the theology and liturgical usages" [12] of the Orthodox people.

Study is an apostolate in itself, because it alone gives a correct concept of the problems. Not only do the Orthodox have erroneous ideas about Catholics; Catholics themselves are poorly informed in respect to the Orthodox. In his encyclical *Ecclesiam dei,* of November 12, 1923, Pius XI noted: "The Latins must acquire a better and deeper knowledge of Eastern matters and usages. An exact knowledge of things will lead to a true appreciation of persons and at the same time a sincere good will towards them. And if they be crowned with Christian charity, these feelings will, by God's grace, be eminently profitable to religious unity." [13] The Pope exhorted the Benedictines along the same vein: "By your words and your writings you shall work to increase zeal for

---

[10] See Aubert, *op. cit.,* p. 110.
[11] Aubert, *ibid.,* p. 111.
[12] Aubert, *ibid.,* p. 111.
[13] Aubert, *ibid.,* p. 106-7.

unity even among Westerners, and to make known the state of the questions that separate the Easterners from us." [14]

The Pope made this petition on the occasion of a "unionistic" congress. Such congresses were being held since 1907 at Velehrad, Czechoslovakia. They consisted in days of historical and theological study. They were held more or less regularly: in 1907, 1909, 1911, 1924, 1927, 1932, and 1936. On the occasion of their resumption in 1924 the Pope wrote to the Bishop of Olmuz, Czechoslovakia. He mentioned the importance of acquiring "new knowledge relative to historical facts and the vicissitudes nations have undergone, the habits and customs of Eastern peoples, and the respective rites and institutions of their Churches." [15] In addressing himself somewhat later to the cardinals in the course of a consistorial allocution, Pius XI urged them to work for unity with the East. "That an attempt of this kind have some chance of achieving results, it is evident that we must, on the one hand, abandon the false idea that has become common in the course of centuries regarding Orthodox institutions and doctrines. On the other hand, we must give ourselves up to a profound study that will show up the agreement between their Fathers and the Latin Fathers, resulting in one and the same faith. In a word, both sides must proceed with mutual exchanges of view in a true spirit of fraternal charity." [16]

Finally, let us quote the distinguished allocution of January 10, 1927, given to the Italian University Catholic Federation. This discourse summarizes Pius XI's entire "Unionistic" program:

> "For reunion it is above all necessary to know one another and to love one another. It is necessary to know one another because it may be said that if the work of reunion has so often failed, these failures have been due in large part to the fact that neither side has known the other. If

---

[14] Aubert, *ibid.*, p. 111-2.
[15] Aubert, *ibid.*, p. 116.
[16] Aubert, *ibid.*, p. 116-7.

there have been mutual prejudices, these prejudices must be resolved. The errors and equivocations that exist and are repeated among the separated brethren against the Catholic Church seem incredible. But on the other hand, Catholics too have sometimes been lacking in a just evaluation of their duty, or because of lack of acquaintance, in friendly devotion. Do we know all the precious, good, and Christian things that these segments of ancient Catholic truth possess? The separated particles of gold-bearing rock themselves contain gold. The venerable Eastern Christian bodies have preserved in their mentality a holiness so worthy of reverence that they not only merit all our respect but likewise our mutual understanding." [17]

These principles may be applied, *mutatis mutandis,* to relations between Catholicism and Protestantism. Pius XI was aware of this himself. In fact he enlarged on this question in a consistorial allocution that he gave on March 24, 1924. This time the Pope called for a similar effort that would include all separated Christians. "We are very grateful to all Catholics," he said, "who, under the inspiration of divine grace, attempt to make it easy for their separated brothers, whoever they may be, to have access to the true faith, by dispelling prejudices and presenting the whole Catholic doctrine to them, and above all by exemplifying in themselves the characteristic sign of Christ's disciples, which is charity." [18] Pius XI encouraged Cardinal Mercier and the Catholics participating in the Malines Conversations.

Pius XI adopted a relatively inflexible position in respect to Protestant ecumenism, however, just like Benedict XV. The "Life and Work" and "Faith and Order" movements did not undertake the long range work of intellectual rapprochements through the study and calm exchanges of information that Pius XI had hoped for. "Life and Work" avoided questions of doctrine, and Pius XI was primarily interested

---

[17] Aubert, *ibid.,* p. 123-4.
[18] Aubert, *ibid.,* p. 103.

in the historical study of doctrine. "Faith and Order" no doubt made doctrinal comparisons, but Pius XI didn't want comparisons, which always remain on the superficial level, but a return to the study of the theology of the Fathers. There was still an apparently unfathomable abyss dividing the "unionism" of Pius XI from the ecumenism of the great Anglican and Protestant movements.

On July 8, 1927, shortly before the Lausanne Conference, the Holy Office recalled the regulation of Benedict XV relative to participation in ecumenical assemblies. On January 6, 1928, after the Conference, the Holy Father published his encyclical *Mortalium animos*. In it he sharply criticized the ecumenical movement for the direction it was taking at the time. Pius XI reproached it with tending to a "Pan-Christianity" established in mutual love but to the disparagement of faith. There is no true unity without the unity of the faith. "Just as charity has an integral and sincere faith as its basis, so unity of faith is the principal means that must unite the disciples of Christ." [19] The encyclical made mention of the fact that Anglican and Protestant Christians are still divided in belief on many points, such as the authority of tradition, the importance of the episcopate and the priesthood, the eucharistic presence, the invocation of saints, and the Blessed Virgin Mary. Then the Pope concluded: "We cannot understand how this wide variation of opinions can open up the way to unity of the Church when this unity can be born of but one single authority, one sole rule of faith, and one identical Christian belief." [20]

Mortalium animos appeared in the same year as *Rerum orientalium*. In it Pius XI censured a move towards unity that suffered from theological shallowness. Then he described the general outline of a safe and calm "unionism." Rejecting a method of union that paid no sufficient attention to the necessary unity of the faith, he preached one that made the

[19] Aubert, *ibid.*, p. 137.
[20] Aubert, *ibid.*, p. 138.

study of doctrine and its development the centre of everything. Many members of the Stockholm and Lausanne Assemblies turned sympathetically towards Rome. They were
undoubtedly disappointed with the encyclical *Mortalium
animos.* Yet if it is put in its historical context and compared
with the numerous documents in which Pius XI tried to
stir up an apostolate for unity, this encyclical is not so
negative as some have thought. It gave a necessary warning:
Catholicism is interested in the ecumenical movement only in
the measure that this involves a return to the evangelical and
traditional sources of faith.

Pius XI's warning did not mean that the Catholic Church
was disinterested in the ecumenical movement as it was. On
the contrary, the Edinburgh and Oxford Assemblies occasioned fruitful contacts. A group of German Catholics published a volume on the theme of the Oxford Conference.[21]
Some English Catholics took part in the preparation of this
very Assembly. Christopher Dawson wrote a chapter on the
kingdom of God and history for one of the preparatory
volumes. Several unofficial Catholic observers went to Oxford
and Edinburgh.

The ecumenical movement learned little by little how to
steer clear of the stumbling-blocks that Pius XI had pointed
out. Protestants and Catholics had not as yet arrived at the
stage of cooperation that Pius XI had enjoined in respect to
the Orthodox Churches. They were beginning to know one
another better, however. As the Sovereign Pontiff had often
said, every path to unity must begin by way of mutual
knowledge and love.

---

[21] Otto Iserland (ed.), *Die Kirche Christi, Grundfragen der
Menschenbildung und Weltgestaltung,* 1937.

CHAPTER XI

MALINES

> *"For nothing in the world would I have one of our*
> *separated brethren say that he confidently knocked at*
> *the door of a Roman Catholic bishop and that this*
> *Roman Catholic bishop refused to receive him."*
> —Cardinal Mercier

Pius XI, being a scholarly man, looked with suspicion on the sensational adventures that the ecumenical assemblies risked becoming. The Catholic ecumenism that was slowly developing during those years was nothing sensational. It was already a matured movement that gave no sign of adolescent enthusiasm. Of course, there were moments of indecision here and there over what method to adopt, and in part, to develop. One remarkable thing about Catholic ecumenism is that it never had a doubtful moment regarding the theological basis of the collective rapprochement of Christians. The mind of Leo XIII was firm on this point from the very beginning. When Pius XI in his turn had to formulate a new direction of Catholic tradition, he was equally sure of it from the very start.

What is said of the Sovereign Pontiffs was equally true of

the theologians. Back in the nineteenth century Abbé Portal already had a clear understanding of the theological exigencies of an apostolate for unity. The theologians of the twentieth century, in pronouncing themselves on the Protestant ecumenical efforts, based themselves on a mature doctrine. Max Pribilla, the pioneer in this field, immediately expounded a mature theology in his book on the first two ecumenical assemblies.[1] It is true that Catholic ecumenism has developed since then, but it has developed along the lines established by its first theologians. It has not experienced the indecisions and repetitions that Protestant ecumenism has passed through. The unity of Catholic doctrine is undoubtedly responsible for this. Since this is so, one cannot help but admire the certitude of Catholic theology at a time when Protestant ecumenism was passing through a crisis of belief in which it evidenced all the rather bungling enthusiasm of adolescence.

This theological sureness was seen at its best at the Malines Conversations. Begun in 1921 under Benedict XV, they continued until 1926 at the rather slow pace of five Conversations in six years. This sound unhurriedness is typical of serious work where efficacy is not measured by the amount of excitement created. It was in keeping with the high intellectual calibre of the exchange of views at Malines, the historical and theological stature of the participants, and the desire of Pius XI to encourage serious intellectual rapprochements.

Anglicans initiated the Malines Conversations. As is already known, the Lambeth Conference of 1920 had launched an appeal for Christian unity. The Anglican bishops at that time reaffirmed the doctrine of the Lambeth Quadrilateral, with which the Christian world was already acquainted. Furthermore, in case the validity of Anglican orders did not satisfy the other Churches, they declared themselves prepared to

---

[1] *Um kirchliche Einheit*, 1929.

receive a supplementary form of ordination should this become necessary for the restoration of Christian unity.

In reality the Anglican bishops were not thinking specifically of the condemnation of their orders by Leo XIII. They had the English Free Churches in mind. Conversations between them and the Anglican Church were in progress. In case of a merger the Anglicans would call for a regularization of the Presbyterian and Congregationalist ministry by their bishops. On the other hand, they declared themselves ready to submit the Anglican ministry to a similar regularization by the Free Churches if it was necessary. The Lambeth Conference therefore had a special situation in mind. But once having admitted the principle of regularization of the ministry, there was no reason to refuse extending it to Rome. Therefore in case of reunion with Rome it is conceivable that by virtue of the Lambeth appeal the Anglican episcopate would submit itself to reordination under conditions laid down by Catholic bishops. This interpretation was a little stretched, but it was made plausible by the Archbishop of Canterbury, Randall Davidson (1848-1930). He himself had forwarded the appeal to some Roman Catholic bishops. A copy had in fact been sent to the Holy Father. In a personal letter to the Archbishop of Canterbury, Cardinal Mercier (1851-1926), Archbishop of Malines, acknowledged receiving the Lambeth appeal.

Lord Halifax, whom we met in 1896 in connection with Anglican ordinations, was still alive. He and Abbé Portal both saw the Anglican bishops' move as a means of again taking up the movement of rapprochement with the Catholic Church in spite of the condemnation of Anglican orders. In effect, if the Anglican clergy consented to be reordained, the condemnation of Anglican orders would no longer be an obstacle to reunion. Lord Halifax got in touch with Cardinal Mercier, who agreed to play host to theological conversations between some Anglicans and some Catholics.

The Malines Conversations were therefore never intended

to negotiate a reunion between Rome and Canterbury. For
one thing, the theologians present were not prepared for
diplomatic transactions. They got together under the eyes
and with the knowledge of their ecclesiastical superiors.
The Archbishop of Canterbury was informed. With the assistance of a few councilors he even prepared the Anglican
contribution to the dialogue. Pius XI sent Cardinal Mercier
his blessing and encouragement. Cardinal Pietro Gasparri,
the secretary of state, wrote Cardinal Mercier that "The
Holy Father authorizes Your Eminence to tell the Anglicans
that he approves and encourages your conversations, and
prays with all his heart that the good God will bless them." [2]
Neither the Anglicans nor the Catholics met as official
representatives. They went as theologians for the purpose of
expressing their personal opinions.

On the other hand, the subject of the Conversations never
pointed towards a union either in the immediate or in the
remote future. Theoretical and dogmatic questions were discussed with no attempt to persuade or convince the other
party, but with the sole purpose of clarification and information. It is true that at the second Conversation the Anglicans, who proposed the program, had put the cart before
the horse so to speak. They wanted to know if and how the
Church of England could unite with Rome while keeping
its traditional privileges, once dogmatic differences were
ironed out. It was a question of discipline and administration
admitting the widest margin possible, but only the supreme
authority itself can give a direct answer to this question.
However, generally they were careful to avoid the merely
possible and they wisely kept to pure theology. The restricted
but very realistic purpose of these Conversations was summarized by Cardinal Mercier as follows: "Our Holy Father
insists particularly that we keep in mind that what he expects
of us above all is a work of rapprochement that consists in

---

[2] See Jacques de Bivort de la Saudée, *Anglicans et Catholiques,*
p. 66-7.

ground-clearing, in reducing friction to a minimum, in relieving both sides of their prejudices, and in reëstablishing the historic truth. Our job is to get rid of obstacles to reunion. The union as such will be wrought by grace at the hour Divine Providence shall see fit to choose." [3] This is the entire ecumenical program in a nutshell.

The discussions that took place at Malines should go down in history. They were unquestionably incomplete but they already bore the stamp of Catholic ecumenism. These meetings had a long-range plan in mind, just as any ecumenism must. But in keeping their theological discussion on the concrete level they were being profoundly realistic.

They adopted the dialogue method. It is well-nigh impossible for large ecumenical assemblies to stimulate a genuine dialogue. The number of participants reaches the thousands and this makes a discussion almost uncontrollable. Besides, the denominational traditions differ too widely to have a true mutual understanding. The Malines meetings, on the other hand, involved two small groups. There were three, then five persons on each side. They were not picked at random but on the basis of their ecumenical experience or theological competence. At the "Faith and Order" meetings it even happened that some delegates confessed their ignorance of the symbols of faith and the early councils. This was not possible with a small, select group. As a matter of fact, Catholic ecumenists have always preferred doctrinal meetings between qualified theologians. The Malines Conversations succeeded in this.

The first Conversation took place in the residence of the Archbishop of Malines from December 6-8, 1921. The three Catholics present were none other than Cardinal Mercier himself, his vicar-general Bishop Van Roey, who later succeeded him as archbishop, and Abbé Portal. There were three Anglicans: Lord Halifax, Walter Frere (1868-1938),

---

3 Bivort, *ibid.,* p. 50.

Bishop of Truro, and Armitage Robinson (1858-1933), Dean of Wells. This was a group of immense prestige, especially since the Bishop of Truro was a liturgist.

These first meetings had been somewhat hastily prepared and had no strictly organized program. Two documents were examined, a memorandum prepared by Halifax and the text of the Lambeth appeal. Halifax's memorandum was brief, and attempted to establish the major points of dispute between Rome and Canterbury from an ecclesiological and sacramental point of view. Halifax was right in noting that "the fundamental question is that of the constitution of the Church." [4] He added that it would be wise to take up this subject only after reaching a theological agreement on other points. Furthermore, no one attempted to underestimate the difficulties during the Malines Conversations. The doctrinal differences within Anglicanism were not forgotten. All the Anglicans present subscribed to a "high church" theology. Yet Halifax wrote Abbé Portal: "It is undeniable that many members of the Church of England would not explain the position and teaching of their Church as I do. Cardinal Mercier must take this fact into consideration. We must admit on our part that we are quite indulgent towards opinions which are in themselves heretical." [5] Keeping these different aspects of Anglicanism in mind, the group studied the nature of the Church, particularly in the light of the decrees of the Councils of Trent and of the Vatican.

The second Conversation, held on March 14-15, 1923, did not share the rather informal character of the first. This time the participants began with a definite subject. This subject, chosen by the Anglicans, was unfortunately extremely complex and not specifically theological. It was concerned with "laying aside dogmatic controversy with a view to con-

---

[4] Jacques de Bivort de la Saudée, *Documents sur le problème de l'union anglo-romaine*, p. 9.

[5] Bivort, *Anglicans*, p. 51.

sidering the possible ways by which, on a practical level, the
Anglican Communion as a body might be joined in a union
with the Holy See which would begin by being more or less
complete; that is, provided some reasonable degree of agreement might first be realized." [6]

As we indicated above, this subject is purely hypothetical.
It cannot lead to exchanges of view that are genuinely fruitful.
Regardless, the Anglicans left satisfied. They had ascertained
at least one thing: if Catholics are uncompromising in doctrine, they are willing to agree to any adjustment whatsoever
of canonical discipline that the hierarchy might see fit to
introduce.

At the third Conversation, November 7-8, 1923, the
number of participants was increased from six to ten. The
Archbishop of Canterbury felt that a variation of Anglo-
Catholicism other than that represented by Lord Halifax
should be represented. He had therefore instructed Charles
Gore and Beresford Kidd to attend the Malines Conversations.
Gore (1853-1932), who was then retired from the bishopric
of Oxford, belonged to the Community of the Resurrection.
He was well known through having inspired the collective
work, *Lux Mundi,* which was responsible for introducing
the science of modern exegesis into Anglo-Catholicism in
1890. He was politely inflexible towards the Catholic Church,
and this made the somewhat timorous Archbishop of Canterbury sure of him. Doctor Kidd (1864-1948) was a man of
vast historical learning.

The number of Catholics was also increased from three
to six. The new participants were chosen for their knowledge
and their reputation. They were Msgr. Pierre Battifol (1861-
1929), who was a Church historian of international repute,
and Canon Hippolyte Hemmer, a specialist in the Fathers of
the Church. Battifol described the spirit in which they went

---

6 Bivort, *Documents,* p. 58-9.

to Malines well when he wrote: "It is no use thinking of a reconciliation of the Anglican Church; that would be utopian; but we can draw nearer to the Anglo-Catholic movement, encourage and enlighten it, perhaps help to detach it from the political or modernistic elements in Anglicanism. That is the perspective in which we must direct our work; conversations without any immediate aim, but helping to make Anglo-Catholic opinion advance in a Catholic direction." [7]

This time the method of discussion was more formal than in the first two Conversations. The Anglicans had prepared theological papers. Reading and discussing them took up all of the two days. Robinson presented a paper on "The Position of Saint Peter in the Primitive Church." Kidd studied "The Use of Texts Pertaining to Saint Peter until around 461." Each paper was followed with long historical commentaries by Battifol. A third essay was read, again by Kidd, on "The Repudiation of the Authority of the Pope by the English Reformation." The Catholics and the Anglicans formulated their separate conclusions on this discussion of the primacy of Rome. They then attempted to determine to what extent these conclusions might agree.

It was necessary to wait one and a half years before the resumption of the Conversations. During the time lag the Malines Conversations were made public. Randall Davidson, the Archbishop of Canterbury, first mentioned them in a pastoral letter on Christmas, 1923. Cardinal Mercier in turn saw fit to set the record straight. On January 18, 1924 he published a pastoral letter on the Malines Conversations. This letter is an authoritative document on the nature of the Catholic apostolate for unity. The Archbishop of Malines described this apostolate as a collective action in view of organic rapprochements. In response to some critics he asserted: "Our method of work seems unsuitable to you.

---

[7] Bivort, *ibid.*, p. 81-2.

Experience has taught you that collective action must be renounced; one must think in terms of individuals. By what law do you limit the action of divine mercy? Do as much as you can for individuals. Do your best to enlighten every soul God puts in your path. Pray for them, devote yourself to them. This is wonderful. No one can criticize you for it. But who authorizes you to shelve collective action? It is your exclusivism that is to be condemned." [8] The Cardinal added that tangible results could not be expected at the present time. All our knowledge and love must nonetheless be put at the disposal of our separated brethren in preparation for collective rapprochements.

The Conversations were resumed on May 19-20, 1925. This time both the Catholic side and the Anglican side had prepared studies. Bishop Van Roey read a paper on "The Episcopate and the Papacy from the Theological Point of View." Doctor Kidd responded with a paper on the same subject. Canon Hemmer read a lengthy study on "The Agreements of the Pope and Bishops from the Historical Point of View." Charles Gore read a memorandum on "Unity in Diversity" that questioned the standards by which dogma developed. Msgr. Battifol answered. Altogether these make up a first-class series of historical studies. It is surprising, therefore, that the fourth Conversation at Malines is known primarily for something else. Cardinal Mercier, referring to the second Conversation, and desiring to complete what had been concluded there, read a paper written by Dom Lambert Bauduin called "The Church of England United, not Absorbed." It was a historical study of the relations that existed between Canterbury and Rome before the Reformation: the conclusion was that it was theoretically possible to recognize a certain independence on the part of the Anglican Church if it were to unite with Rome. There was no extended

---

[8] Bivort, *ibid.*, p. 148.

discussion on this point, however. The essay in question was not considered officially part of the Conversation.

Cardinal Mercier died on January 23, 1926. Then Abbé Portal passed away on the following June 20th. The Malines Conversations could not continue as they were without these two great men. A fifth Conversation held on October 11-12, 1926, was the last of the Malines Conversations. Lord Halifax, Kidd and Frere came over from England. The Catholics were Bishop Van Roey, now promoted to the Archbishopric of Malines, Battifol, and Hemmer. There was really nothing new about this meeting. The members were content with reviewing the work of the preceding Conversations. Two summaries had been prepared, and they spent most of their time examining these.

How should we assess the value of the Malines Conversations? The historical and theological importance of the information revealed by the Anglican and the Catholic participants alike must be fully recognized. And Cardinal Mercier must be praised for his generosity. He made the meetings possible and was largely responsible for the friendly atmosphere in which they took place. The Cardinal knew that the apostolate for unity must fuse theological science, steadfastness in doctrine, a sincere explanation of the faith, friendliness towards men, and the mutual understanding necessary for grasping the religious situation of separated Christians.

The participants of the Malines Conversations enjoyed an advantage that ecumenical workers do not always have. The doctrines at issue were not far apart. There is less distance between Anglo-Catholicism and Catholicism than there is between Anglo-Catholicism and the "low church" theologians within Anglicanism itself. Under these conditions the dialogue proceeded rather smoothly. Now and then Charles Gore made the situation uneasy with his bold anti-papalism.

But anything can be said without offense if the participants feel that the speaker is guided solely by love for the truth.

The Malines Conversations taught therefore a lesson. It is simply that *dialogue* between members of the Catholic Church and members of the separated Confessions *is possible*. What Irish Bishop Doyle dreamed of back in 1824 was subjected to the test of experience at Malines. As would be expected, the facts proved that Doyle was right. Dialogue between Anglicans and Catholics is the best way of reconciling minds in truth and hearts in charity.

The experience also proves that this sort of meeting, limited both in the importance and in the number of participants, is the ideal form of ecumenical dialogue. Protestant ecumenists were negotiating important projects at this time that led up to the excited atmosphere of the great Assemblies of Stockholm, Lausanne, Oxford and Edinburgh. These large-scale events were much more effective in stirring up peoples' minds than modest exchanges of viewpoint. But in the long run the work of small committees goes more deeply. The organizers of the great movements are themselves aware that a big conference would amount to nothing without committee labor. The Malines Conversations in their unhurried style, without aiming at results, without any personal advantage whatever except for the immense benefit of knowing one another better, form the standard type of ecumenical dialogue.

Finally, the Malines Conversations made Catholics think about the ecumenical problem. There were many misunderstandings. Cardinal Mercier's intentions were sometimes misrepresented. He justified himself masterfully in his pastoral letter of January, 1924. In it he pointed out the existence and necessity of an apostolate for unity which is not directed towards individual conversions, but towards rapprochement with Churches and doctrines. Nothing in ecumenical literature has ever surpassed what Cardinal Mercier wrote at that time. "For nothing in the world would I have one of our separated

brethren say that he confidently knocked at the door of a
Roman Catholic bishop and that this Roman Catholic bishop
refused to receive him." [9] What the Cardinal said in reference
to a bishop applies to every Catholic. This is Catholic
ecumenism.

---

[9] Bivort, *ibid.*, p. 146.

CHAPTER XII

UNA SANCTA

> *"Does what we have been saying mean that in the event*
> *of a reunion the Catholic is to remain in undisputed*
> *possession of his beliefs, whereas the Protestant is to*
> *abandon and even deny those truths which are char-*
> *acteristic of his religion and especially dear to him? . . .*
> *The question of reunion stands or falls by our answer*
> *to it."*
>
> —Karl Adam

While the Conversations between Anglicans and Catholics were underway at Malines, the foundations were being laid in Germany for a rapprochement between Lutherans and Catholics. There were precedents in Germany, the land of Moehler and of the theological renewal of the nineteenth century. It was also the seat of the most recent schism, that of the Old Catholics. The religious situation in Germany was nevertheless favorable to a rapprochement between separated Christians.

In the first place, German Protestantism was not divided up into innumerable Churches like American Protestantism, for example. The Lutheran tradition is predominant, though there are also a number of Calvinist Churches. Homogeneity of this sort facilitates rapprochements. Here as elsewhere, union invites union. It is easier for Catholics to understand a united than a divided Protestantism. It is more feasible for them to enter into a dialogue with a steady, stable partner than with a many-sided partner.

In the second place, German Protestantism is a doctrinal confessionalism. Its Lutheran origin provides it with fixed doctrinal bases, as found in the Lutheran "confessional books." Adopted as a principle of agreement between the Lutheran Churches towards the end of the sixteenth century, these books are still the traditional source of reference for Lutheranism.[1] Of course, Lutherans refer to Holy Scripture as the sole source of faith, but they always read Scripture in the light of a doctrinal tradition that is essentially contained in the confessional books inherited from the sixteenth century. In the nineteenth century Germany was, evidently, affected by Protestant liberalism. Certain modern theologians like Rudolf Bultmann are still largely dependent on a somewhat outdated liberalism where tradition and traditional doctrines lose their importance. On the whole, however, modern German Lutheranism has rejected the temptation of Protestant liberalism. A Catholic always feels more at ease with Protestants who are concerned about doctrine than with those who are mainly interested in action. Certainly, Catholicism is a way of life and a sacramental experience, but this way of living and this experience are inseparable from doctrine. The Catholic is consequently able to talk with Protestants who have a solid theology. A similar dialogue with Protestants who have no theology or whose theology is too much characterized by the naturalism and rationalism of liberal Protestantism would be impossible.

There is a third reason why Germany should be the choice spot for Catholic ecumenism. In some countries Catholics and Protestants rub shoulders without making any contact.

---

[1] These books are: The Augsburg Confession, Luther's two Catechisms, the Schmalkalde Articles, and the Book of Concord.

They live next to each other but draw up into their shells as soon as anybody talks about religion. Catholics and Protestants of the same nation are tempted to ignore one another, at least if suffering has not taught them the need for being friendly. But the experience of national socialism showed the Christians of Germany that they needed one another. As we know, Catholicism was cunningly pursued by Hitler's regime. The same was true of Lutheranism and Calvinism. By means of a truly diabolical scheme the Nazi leaders even tried to pervert the Gospel among the Protestants and to create a new German Church. This was started in April, 1933, by the organization of the self-styled "German Christians," led by the "bishop of the Reich," Ludwig Müller (1883-1946). The "protests of Barmen" on May 31, 1934, saved the Christian substance of Lutheranism. The German Protestant resistance to Hitlerian paganism became known by the noble name of the Confessing Church. Confessing Protestantism and Catholicism were both persecuted in those days. Persecution, in turn, brought Catholics and Protestants together. This has had a profound effect on German Christianity.

Finally, the way that German universities are organized favors interconfessional meetings. In many countries the universities keep a strict line of division between theology and the academic disciplines. Germany has not made this regrettable division. Most of the large universities have one and sometimes two departments of theology. Heidelberg has a department of Protestant theology and Munich has a department of Catholic theology. Tübingen has both. The consequence is that the professors and students of the departments of theology are in contact with their colleagues in other departments. This tends to create an openness of mind and method that facilitates cultural interchange. German religious culture is therefore open to philosophical thought and intellectual currents of all descriptions. Theological culture as such remains faithful to the two major German Confessions, Catholicism and Lutheranism. There is mutual interchange even when no dialogue is in session. This is fertile soil for the growth of germinal seeds of rapprochement of thought such as ecumenism feeds on.

The man who was to unite the scattered children of the *Una Sancta* movement appeared on the scene shortly after the First World War. Meetings between Protestants and Catholics increased considerably after the War ended. It was particularly during the national socialist persecution that Catholics and Protestants got together for consultation. They had occasional meetings that were loosely organized. Circumstances forced them to face the same dangers together. Father Max Joseph Metzger (1887-1944) launched the idea of turning evil into good by organizing a brotherhood movement among separated Christians.

Max Joseph Metzger had founded a religious congregation called the "League of the White Cross," subsequently called the "Society of Christ the King." Established at Graz in Austria in 1919, the foundation was transferred to Germany. It was then that Father Metzger founded the *Una Sancta* brotherhood. His plan was to channel the vague desires that Protestants and Catholics had for getting together. Influential Lutherans like Friedrich Heiler gladly supported this movement, already well on the way. *Una Sancta* was a "free and voluntary society that did not question the members' religious freedom and imposed no external obligation." The members prayed for peace between Christians and worked to establish and maintain concord. Metzger summarized it thus:

"The members undertake to pray, using the Lord's Prayer common to all Christians, and also the high-priestly prayer of Christ, for the coming of the kingdom of Christ on earth, and for its unity in faith and love, and to urge such prayer on their fellow-Christians. They will endeavour to build bridges, intellectual and spiritual, between the separated Christian Confessions, emphasizing that which unites rather than that which divides; clearing away misunderstandings; honouring the truth in all, deepening brotherly love, and seeking to promote brotherly intercourse and common service in tasks of Christian helpfulness."

Local meetings between Catholics and Protestants were followed by two congresses, in 1939 and 1940. The Second World War put an end to these gatherings. Metzger's activity, plus the fact that he held to a pacifist position, made the national socialist authorities suspicious of him, apostle of peace that he was. After a number of temporary arrests he was finally condemned to death for "treason." He was executed on April 17, 1944.

During one of his prison terms, in the autumn of 1939, Metzger wrote down his ideas on Christian reunion. He wrote a letter to Pope Pius XII. It is hard to determine whether this letter was addressed to the Holy Father merely as a literary device, or was actually sent to him. Whatever the case may be, the letter is worth being known. It summarizes in a few lines what many Catholic ecumenists have found to be true in their relations with Protestants.[2]

Max Metzger first of all speaks of the international situation. It is the first month of the War. "The need of our day" he says, "through which God is speaking to us—imperatively demands the utmost effort to heal the dismemberment of the Christian Church, to make Christ's kingdom of peace effectual throughout the world." After mentioning the close relations that he has with many Protestants, Metzger concludes:

"With my knowledge of the mentality of those outside the Church I may say that it is far less differences of dogma than difficulties of a spiritual nature which prevent a close approach of the other Communions to the Roman Catholic Church."

He then quotes some of the accusations made against the Church. They amount to an accusation of pride. Metzger

---

[2] The entire text in English is in Lillian Stephenson's biography, *Max Josef Metzger*, 1952, pp. 44-55.

then gets to the main point of his letter and to the core of the ecumenical problem. The entire passage follows:

"Nothing would more effectually remove these prejudices, and thereby promote an inward drawing nearer of the religious Communions separated from us, than the honest, humble attitude, proceeding from within outward, of all bishops and pastors despite, or even because of, their responsibility for carrying out their apostolic calling. Anyone who is familiar with the inner development of the Churches separated from us will admit the truth of the following statement, that dogmatic differences—however serious and important—are not today the main element which hinders reunion. Much more important is the spiritual attitude on both sides. This cannot be settled merely by speaking of 'truth' on the one side and 'error' on the other, for it has often to do with tensions which are soluble only in the universality of the one Church such as: God or Man? Christ or the Church? Written Word or Tradition? Grace or Works? Law or Liberty? Justice or Love? Letter or Spirit? Law or Gospel? A Sacramental or a Spiritual Religion? Popular Piety or Higher Mysticism? A National Church or a World Church? While actual differences have far more to do with theological opinions and questions of church discipline than with 'the faith once revealed' concerning which the Church 'as pillar and ground of the truth' (I Tim. 3:15) is unable to make concessions, it is evident that it is in the discussion of these very questions that deep humility and sympathetic love are specially necessary, if we are not to cling to our personal opinions and to historic developments which, though they may flatter human sensitiveness, yet are capable of, or need, examination under the guidance of the Holy Spirit."

Max Metzger ended his letter to the Pope by suggesting the convocation of an ecumenical council to put an end to Christian separations. He envisaged a council that would be prepared by "confidential talks" between Catholics and Protestants. While he was under no illusion about the amount of time such a rapprochement would take, he saw it as the only hope of reunion: "I know that it is more than can be hoped for, but it seems to me that only a great gesture of faith, humility and of love can resolve the problem of the fate of Christianity. The history of the Church and that of the world as well will raise up a monument to the Pope who starts this work on a large scale and to the one who completes it later on."

This perhaps prophetic vision did not die with the execution of Max Metzger. The work of *Una Sancta* continued and grew under his immediate successor, Father Matthias Laros, then under Dom Thomas Sartory. Laros developed its principles and their application in a book called *Schöpferischer Friede der Konfessionen* (1950). Sartory applied these principles in his study of the ecumenical movement, *Die oeckumenische Bewegung und die Einheit der Kirche* (1955).[3] *Una Sancta* changed from the status of a confraternity of prayer to that of a "movement." Under this new form *Una Sancta* organized a number of meetings and conventions immediately after the War. We are indebted to one of them, held in Stuttgart in 1947, for Karl Adam's *One and Holy*. Let us read the lines where Karl Adam describes the spirit of the *Una Sancta* movement: "We must each take our own Confession seriously; we must each give ourselves unconditionally to Christ and His Holy will; and, inspired by this love of Christ, we must each root out of ourselves all loveless prejudices against those of the other faith. These tasks in the religious and moral order are the necessary *a priori* preliminaries to any union between us, to any approach between Catholics and Protestants if it is to bear fruit." [4]

The *Una Sancta* movement has lost a little of the popularity that it enjoyed just after the War. Actually, Germany's

---

[3] Also, Hans Asmussen and Thomas Satory, *Gesprach Zurischen de Konfessionen,* 1959.

[4] *One and Holy,* p. 111.

present situation helps meetings between Catholics and Protestants progress in the direction of a more profound doctrinal study. Archbishop Lorenz Jaeger has established the Johann Moehler Institute at Paderborn. Its purpose is to study ecumenism and Protestantism from the Catholic viewpoint. Archbishop Jaeger also serves as delegate of the German hierarchy for matters concerning inter-denominational problems. Dom Emmanuel Heufelder, abbot of the Benedictine Abbey of Niederaltaich in Bavaria, has introduced his abbey to ecumenical work. Dom Thomas Sartory, the present director of the *Una Sancta* movement, also edits the *Una Sancta* review. From an occasional paper giving news of the movement, it has become progressively since 1950 a theological review of the highest quality where Catholics and Protestants are engaged in a constant dialogue. *Catholica,* another theological review that is solely devoted to ecumenical problems, should also be mentioned. It was founded by Robert Grosche and is now published by the Johann Moehler Institute.

One more fact should be known. German Catholic ecumenism does not work only in the irenic atmosphere of *Una Sancta.* Thus the ecumenical chronicles that appear in the monthly bulletin of information and documentation, *Herder-Korrespondenz,* preserve often enough a somewhat polemic flavor. Doctor Karlheinz-Schmidthuis, who directs the chronicle, is well informed on, and sympathetic towards, the ecumenical cause. Nevertheless *Herder-Korrespondenz* occasionally comes out with comparisons or reflections that are not always in the best spirit of brotherhood. The same may be said of what J. P. Michael writes, whether as a contributor to periodicals, or in certain pages of his very useful and well written book, *Christen suchen eine Kirche* (1958).

German Catholic ecumenism must be related to the intensive ecumenical activity in Holland. Holland is possibly the only country where prayer for reunion with the Orthodox Churches is so popular as to be represented in many parishes. It is certainly the only one where the bishops have assigned a considerable number of priests to an ecumenical apostolate of friendly meetings and unbiased interest. In 1958 one of them told me that more than a hundred priests were occupied in this work. These priests are mostly located in the dechristianized regions of North Holland and in the recovered provinces of Zuyder Zee. Their apostolate includes the mission of evangelizing people who were formerly Calvinists and are now agnostic, and that of fraternizing among Protestant Christians. This entire apostolate is directed by the episcopal delegate, Monsignor Willebrands. Msgr. Willebrands acts also as the secretary for an inter-European group, the "Catholic Conference for Ecumenical Questions." [5] He is therefore in a perfect position to see that this apostolate remains truly ecumenical in spirit. There are also active centers for theological meetings between Dutch Reformed Church ministers and Catholic theologians. We may at least mention Father Radboud Weel, who directs such a centre at Laren, near Hilversum.

Since 1948 the Institute of Byzantine Studies at Niemegen has published a quarterly review, *Het Christelijk Oosten en Hereniging,* that is specially devoted to the problems of Eastern Orthodoxy. It also keeps its readers up-to-date on world-wide ecumenical developments by means of news reports and articles. Besides this, Holland has undertaken pioneer work in another area related to ecumenism. The Catholic University of Niemegen was the first to establish a chair of Protestant studies. It set an example that has been followed by others. But there are still too few chairs for the study of Protestantism in Catholic institutes and universities. There still isn't any in France at this date.

Catholic ecumenism in Holland has therefore produced works of very high interest. It has not developed a new theoretical approach. Drawing its inspiration from the best

---

[5] Since these lines were written, Msgr. Willebrands has been appointed by Pope John XXIII secretary of a commission for Ecumenical matters headed by Cardinal Bea.

that German and French theology have to offer in the matter
of ecumenism, it has derived some concrete applications from
them adaptable to the situation in their country. This may be
considered the ideal to emulate, taking differences of mentality
and of situations into account.

The good will of Dutch Protestants does not adequately
account for this abundance of ecumenical enterprises. Dutch
Protestantism is divided into two principal Churches, the
Hervormde, which has more members and is the more
liberal, and the *Gereformeerde,* which has fewer members
and is more conservative. Both of them are Calvinist. There,
as elsewhere, the German occupation and spiritual resistance
to Nazism brought Catholics and Protestants together. In 1950
the general synod of the Reformed Church (Hervormde)
made an accusation against Catholics, rightly or wrongly:
"The Catholic Church has very rapidly and very deliberately
returned to its isolation with the purpose of using all sorts of
means to increase its influence on the nation's life." [6] This
synod wasted no time. It published a long pastoral letter,
dated March 23, 1950, presented as "the beginning of a new
reflection of our Church concerning major issues on which
the Reformation Churches must always oppose Rome in the
name of the Gospel." [7] This letter proceeded with a detailed
study of Catholic doctrine, opposed point by point to "the
Gospel." The French translation is 155 pages long, which
gives some indication of the extent of this study. No doubt
Catholic doctrine is oftentimes wrongly interpreted in it and
its interpretations of the Gospel should be treated cautiously.
The important thing here is to know that an invariably
harmonious atmosphere between Catholics and Protestants
is not strictly necessary for the development of ecumenical
thought and activity on the part of Catholics. Ecumenism can
and must be born, even with all the frictions that one side

---

[6] *Catholicisme et Protestantisme. Lettre pastorale du synode general de l'Eglise réformée des Pays-Bas,* 1957, p. 8.
[7] *Ibid.,* p. 5.

or the other may produce. Its function is to clear up the atmosphere and create a good will that will not be wrecked by circumstances and in periods of unusual stress. Holland's experience is an example for all in this respect.

This study of the contribution made by Germany and Holland to present-day Catholic ecumenism can be brought to a close here. We have disregarded one aspect, however. A short history of ecumenism cannot give an account of all the recent theological activities that for one reason or other are of ecumenical interest. But German and French theology take the lead in this area, as in others. German theologians are inclined towards the study of Protestantism. We are indebted to them for some of the best modern studies written by Catholics. Joseph Lortz, of the University of Mainz, has revived the study of Martin Luther among Catholics. Max Pribilla opened the way to the study of Protestant ecumenism with his previously mentioned work on the Stockholm and Lausanne Assemblies. The German and Austrian proponents of "kerygmatic theology" have been indirectly responsible for bringing Catholic thought near to the Lutheran concern for the Word. As founder of the review *Catholica,* which he directed until 1957, Robert Grosche deserves special mention among those who have been very specially devoted to "questions of controversy" between Catholics and Protestants. Also deserving of recognition are Joseph Geiselmann, of the University of Tübingen, and Heinrich Fries, in particular for his work on Karl Barth and Rudolf Bultmann.[8] Among the German-speaking Swiss we will single out two specialists in the theology of Barth: Hans Urs von Balthasar [9] of Basel, and Hans Küng [10] of Zurich, at present professor at the University of Münster. Among the Dutch, W.H. van de Pol, who

---

[8] *Bultmann, Barth und die katholische Theologie,* 1955; Fries also took up a dialogue with Asmussen in *Antwort an Asmussen,* 1959.

[9] *Karl Barth, Darstellung und Deutung seine Theologie,* 1951.

[10] *Rechtfertigung. Die Lehre Karl Barthe und eine katholische Besinnung,* 1957.

holds the chair of "Protestant phenomenology" at the University of Niemegen, deserves recognition. [11]

We see then that in the Germanic countries Catholic ecumenism is not a temporary or superficial rapprochement. It has taken on a large-scale work that consists in achieving a common outlook by means of study as well as of prayer. Catholic theology can become capable of engaging in an intelligent dialogue with the best of Lutheran and Calvinist theology only at the cost of long hours of study. From here on the way is reasonably clear, thanks to the enlightening work of German Catholicism.

[11] *The Christian Dilemma*, 1952; *Das reformatorische Christentum*, 1956.

CHAPTER **XIII**

SPIRITUAL ECUMENISM

> *"The time has not yet come for the work of theologians and superiors, but it is time for psychological purification by means of prayer, kindness, mutual esteem of individuals and of all their human and Christian values, all the sweet fruits of charity."*
>
> —Paul Couturier

Catholic ecumenism has grown simultaneously in numerous countries or groups of countries. It has not followed the same pattern of growth everywhere. Its groundwork varies, both in respect to theology and experience. While the foundations of the *Una Sancta* movement were being laid in Germany, the Malines Conversations evidenced a mature ecumenical method. Yet this high quality of ecumenical thought and action were not universal in France. On the French side, the Malines Conversations were entirely the work of Abbé Portal, a veteran of the Church unity problem. He was assisted by wise, competent, and generous collaborators, but neither Canon Hemmer nor Bishop Battifol were especially experienced in the problem of severed Christianity. On the Belgian side, the Conversations were the work of Cardinal Mercier.

He was no specialist in Anglicanism or ecumenism. It was his generosity and his quick comprehension of the problems and their solution that permitted him to control the debates. All this does not mean that Catholic ecumenism spread quickly throughout Belgium and France.

A significant current of thought interested itself in Church union however, especially with regard to the Orthodox Church. It is important to know how it developed. During the reign of Napoleon III French political interests were centered in the East. The Crimean War had brought public attention to what was subsequently referred to as the "Eastern question." It was mainly a question of knowing what would be the ruling power in Eastern Europe and the Near East after the anticipated downfall of the Ottoman Empire. The Russian Empire stuck to its traditional policy regarding this part of the Mediterranean. France, dreaming of being once more protector of the Holy Places, also had its eyes on it. Church interests rather quickly turned in the same direction. The "Eastern question" had a religious aspect.

In 1861 the question of the reunion of the Bulgarian Orthodox with the Roman Communion was in the air. In fact, an act of union was signed. Bishop Sokolsky was consecrated "uniate" bishop on April 8, 1861. But the bishop disappeared the following June 18th, evidently kidnapped by Russian agents. He ended his days in a Russian monastery, apparently faithful to the act of union to the last.

The disappearance of the bishop marked the end of that union. But Pius IX, desiring to strengthen the few Catholic centers of the Byzantine Rite, decided to send some French religious. In 1863 Father Emmanuel d'Alzon (1810-80), founder of the Augustinians of the Assumption, made a trip to Istanbul and Bulgaria. After that he sent religious to Bulgaria, Turkey, and in 1903, to Russia.

Father d'Alzon's ideas and the principles he wanted to apply were not ecumenical in the modern sense of the word. In 1862 he wrote: "The thought of attacking the entire

Photian schism seems splendid to me, but what an undertaking!" [1] This is the lofty language of an apostle. It is not
yet that of an apostle of ecumenism. Father d'Alzon thought
in terms of the gradual disappearance of the Byzantine Rite.
In a memorandum sent to Pope Pius IX on April 25, 1863,
he even mentioned "the necessity of working for the absorp-
tion of the Eastern Rites by the Latin Rite." [2]

On the other hand, since Father d'Alzon was native to the
Nimes region, he was well up on Protestant developments.
He was above all impressed by the doctrinal decadence of
liberal Protestantism. In regard to Protestantism he envisaged
an apostolate whose method is "primarily apologetic. It has
conversions first in mind, but includes ecumenical elements
in the true sense of the word: prayers, retreat houses, and
above all, the testimony of a truly Christian life." [3]

As it turned out, the method gradually improved. It tended
more and more towards a true ecumenical attitude, particularly in regard to Orthodoxy. In 1893 a great eucharistic
congress was organized at Jerusalem with the avowed purpose of making the Latin Catholics better acquainted with
the Eastern Rites and of affording Catholics and Orthodox
an opportunity to have a friendly meeting. Actually though,
the Eastern question was posed in over-simplified terms.
People commonly thought that Orthodoxy amounted to a
question of rite and liturgical language. They have had to
learn since that a rite is but an exterior manifestation of a
deeper reality. Above all, Orthodoxy is faithful to a theology
and a tradition that are more characterized by patristic
thought than by Latin theology, which is dominated by medi-

---

[1] Quoted by Vitalien Laurent, *Le Père d'Alzon et le problème du
retour à l'unité catholique des Eglises greco-slaves*, in *Mélanges
Emmanuel d'Alzon*, 1951, p. 287. The entire article may be read,
pp. 283-301. See also Tavard, *The Assumptionists and the work for
Christian unity*, in the *Eastern Churches Quarterly*, 1950, pp. 428-94.

[2] *Ibid.*, p. 299.

[3] Olaf Hendricks, *Le père d'Alzon et les dissidences occidentales*,
ibid., p. 278.

eval scholasticism. Considering the means that were at their disposal, the effort of the Assumption Fathers was remarkable for its breadth. In 1897 Father Louis Petit (1868-1927), who became the Latin Archbishop of Athens in 1917, started a scientific review concerned with Byzantine history and the Orthodox Churches. First styled "Echoes of the East," it is now called "Review of Byzantine Studies." It is published by the French Institute of Byzantine Studies, which was established at Istanbul in 1897 by Louis Petit and transferred to Bucharest in 1937 and to Paris in 1946. This Institute is dedicated to an objective and disinterested study of Byzantine religious history with no ulterior apologetic motive. It provided the Oriental Institute, established in Rome by Benedict XV, with some of its first professors.

In 1922 the Assumption Fathers founded a quarterly review in France that was a pioneer endeavour in the spreading of ecumenical ideas. At first it was called "The Church Union" and kept abreast of Orthodox and Catholic news in the Christian East. In 1930 its name was changed to "Church Unity" and in 1938 it ceased publication. This review simply gave the news and subscribed to no ecumenical theories. Factual knowledge is indispensable for any kind of apostolate. Knowledge of the facts is alone capable of nourishing prayer and stimulating creative ideas that will give rise to great undertakings.

The disappearance of "Church Unity" in 1938 represented the turning of a page in the history of French ecumenism. Up until that time the East was at the center of things. French Protestantism was thought to be decadent and was therefore not at the forefront. In the East itself there were two issues at work. Firstly, the problem was to strengthen the position of the Eastern "Uniates," i.e., Byzantine Rite Catholics. Secondly, scholars devoted themselves to the study of Byzantine history. They were engaged in an eminently ecumenical work.

Unionism of the first type, which depends mainly on the

Catholic Churches of the Eastern Rite, is not expressly ecumenical. Reconciliations of so-called "Uniate" groups can be but partial reunions. They cannot solve the problem of schism as a whole. Study has another scope. Intellectual dialogues were undertaken with the Orthodox under the aegis of science and history. The aforementioned Velehrad Congresses, held between 1907 and 1936 with the encouragement of the Sovereign Pontiffs, were theological assemblies where views were exchanged in a spirit of objective study and Christian brotherhood.

Desires for Church union spread somewhat haphazardly, then, but in a spirit of generosity. The foundations of an ecumenical deepening were then laid by the Benedictine Order. Due to Pius XI and Dom Fidelis von Stotzingen, Primate of the Order of St. Benedict, the Priory of Amay-sur-Meuse was founded in 1925. It was a bi-ritual monastery with Latin Rite and Byzantine Rite monks. The assigned task of this foundation was to work for rapprochement among Christians, especially between Catholics and Orthodox. The founder and first prior of Amay was Dom Lambert Bauduin. He was a friend of Cardinal Mercier.

Dom Lambert Bauduin gave a distinctly ecumenical orientation to the Amay community that was in line with the intentions of Pius XI. The review "Irenikon," started in 1927, included and still includes informative reports on ecumenical activities throughout the world, together with theological and historical articles of great significance. Dom Bauduin insisted that an extensive psychological preparation was necessary before Christians could envisage reunion. And this preparation had to be spiritual. No unity is possible without prayer.[4] Being at the same time a theological center, Amay wanted to become a center of spirituality. They consecrated two special periods to prayer for unity, the nine days preceding Pentecost, instituted by Leo XIII, and in January, the octave be-

---

[4] See Dom Lambert Bauduin, *L'Oeuvre des Moines Bénédictins d'Amay-sur-Meuse*, 1925.

tween the Feast of St. Peter's Chair at Rome (Jan. 8) and the Feast of the Conversion of St. Paul (Jan. 25). Besides this, Amay was a center of hospitality and friendly meetings for those who were dedicated to the cause of Christian unity.

It was due precisely to a sojourn at Amay that the great French apostle of ecumenism found his vocation. Abbé Paul Couturier (1881-1935) was a priest of the Diocese of Lyon and a professor in a school in that city. Being already in contact with the Orthodox through his work with Russian refugees of Lyons, he spent a month at Amay in 1932. He went home determined to introduce the January Octave of Prayer to Lyons.

The January Octave was of Anglican origin. Two Anglican ministers began the practice in 1908. One of them, Spencer Jones (1857-1943), was English. The idea of a prayer for unity with Rome originated with him. The other, Lewis Wattson (1863-1940), was an American. He selected the date for this prayer. Spencer Jones always remained an Anglican, praying to the end for the return of his Church to Catholic unity. Lewis Wattson, the founder of a religious congregation, became a Roman Catholic towards the end of 1908. Under the name of Father Paul he popularized the prayer in Catholicism that he and his friend had begun in Anglicanism. The purpose that was then assigned to the Chair of Unity Octave as it is called, was the conversion of all separated Christians to Rome. Pope Pius X, Benedict XV and Pius XI had encouraged this pious practice.

It was soon evident to Abbé Couturier that the Unity Octave called for a special psychological preparation if it was to conserve its original character of prayer for separated Christians. Through recurrent insistence on return to the Roman fold, the majority of separated Christians were in fact excluded. One prayed *for* them, but not *with* them for Christian unity. Abbé Couturier therefore set himself to expanding the spirit of the Octave of Prayer in order to make it truly ecumenical. "Neither Catholic prayer, nor Orthodox prayer, nor Anglican prayer, nor Protestant prayer suffice. All of them are necessary, and all of them together." [5] Couturier published these ideas in an article of *Revue Apologetique* in 1935 entitled "For Christian unity; the psychology of the January 18-25th Octave of Prayer."

Abbé Couturier immediately gained a large audience of French-speaking Catholics. This audience was to increase. Under its new form the January Octave of Prayer spread to most of the larger cities. Its first name was gradually replaced by a new title: "The week of universal prayer of Christians for Christian unity." Approved by the Reformed Church of France in its 1936 synod, it gained many Protestant parishes. At the same time, the prayer week spread beyond the boundaries of France. The spirit of Abbé Couturier was too close to that of the *Una Sancta* movement that had already started in Germany not to get a friendly reception from German Catholics. The prayer for unity such as Couturier had conceived it won over a number of Anglican circles from the very start. It soon penetrated Protestantism in Sweden, Holland, and elsewhere.

Like Max Metzger, Paul Couturier kept up a voluminous correspondence with all parts of the Christian world. He was not much of a writer; he never published a single book. He was content with articles and a few short pamphlets. But he was a tireless letter writer: his ecumenical apostolate took on the friendly direction followed in his correspondence. He had numerous personal contacts with Protestants and Anglicans. He made most of them during his visits to Great Britain. Together with some Catholic colleagues he organized meetings with Anglicans and Protestants of several days' duration, usually in Switzerland and France. These meetings were half-way retreats, half-way exchanges of theological views. While he favoured spiritual contacts first of all, Coutu-

---

[5] Quoted by Maurice Villain, *L'abbé Paul Couturier, Apôtre de l'Unité Chrétienne,* 1957, p. 57.

rier by no means excluded theological discussion and information.

Through these numerous contacts in person or by letter, Abbé Couturier became acutely aware of the Orthodox, Anglican and Protestant mentality. This helped him deepen his conception of ecumenism. His pamphlets *Rapprochements entre Chrétiens au XXe siècle* (1944) and *L'Unité chrétienne et la prière* (reprinted in 1955) present his views at their best. Couturier was aware of the fact that the "Catholic Church is not alone in believing that it alone possesses the truth," and of the contingent fact that "psychologically one's own faith and that of others are strictly identical," both in respect to Catholics and to others as well.[6] If everyone is supposed to pray for the same Christian unity, then it is necessary that the goal be fixed apart from denominational differences. No one need renounce his own faith. The Catholic firmly believes that there is no complete unity apart from the Bishop of Rome, successor of Peter. But he ought to pray, not directly for a conversion or a return, but that all Christians might grow spiritually. Only such a growth will enable them to perceive and accept Christ's will for His Church. The "maturity of Christian groups"[7] is a condition for unity. "Christian unity will be attained," prophesied Couturier, "when the praying Christ finds enough Christian souls in all denominations so that He Himself can freely pray to His Father for unity."[8] Abbé Couturier therefore wanted to arouse a prayerful ecumenism, which he himself referred to as "spiritual emulation." He did not want confusion, indifferentism or inter-denominationalism, but that all work alongside one another, "a parallel march of Christian communities towards the unity that Christ wants His Church to have."[9]

---

[6] Villain, *ibid.*, p. 167.
[7] *Rapprochements entre les chrétiens au XXe siècle*, p. 37.
[8] *L'Unité Chrétienne et la prière*, p. 20.
[9] *Ibid.*, p. 17.

Abbé Couturier welcomed all evidences of the anxiety for
unity as so many signs of spiritual emulation in the making.
He wrote of Protestant ecumenism: "It is a serious mistake to
think that ecumenism is anti-Roman, the work of a group
that is 'in opposition' to Rome. Such an attitude implies an
ignorance of ecumenism, due to not going back to the sources.
Whoever studies it faithfully sees it as a great gift of the
Holy Spirit for the reintegration of severed Christianity. Let
us not fail to recognize the gift of the Spirit." [10] Writing about
the Prayer Octave as it was before acquiring this new form,
he said: "Let us learn to admire God's works and how to
thank Him." [11] This is no narrow attitude but a generous-
hearted viewing of the works of the Spirit.

Abbé Couturier's work continues. In Lyons itself tracts
and posters for the week of the Prayer Octave appear every
year under the auspices of Father P. Michalon. Father Maurice Villain, an intimate friend and the biographer of Abbé
Couturier, makes spiritual ecumenism known on the theological level through his articles and lectures. His book *Introduction à l'Oecuménisme* (1958) explains his own ecumenical
experience along the pattern of Abbé Couturier. In this
book he describes ecumenism as a "new prophecy" [12] that,
in the midst of Christian divisions, anticipates the renewed
unity that is clearly visible to the eyes of the whole world.

The figure of Abbé Couturier still dominates French
Catholic ecumenism. This can not simply be identified with
Couturier and his followers, however. Ecumenism was already in process of formation before his time. The work
undertaken by the "Church Unity" review ceased shortly
before the Second World War. But the same tendencies and
currents reappeared after the War. In 1945 Father Charles
Boyer founded the *Unitas* association in Rome. It publishes

---

[10] I find these lines, handwritten by Abbé Couturier himself, on
the bottom of pages 18 and 19 of my copy of *Rapprochements entre
les chrétiens au XXe siècle.*

[11] *Rapprochements*, p. 31.

[12] *Introduction à l'Oecuménisme*, p. 229.

a review, *Unitas,* that appears in Italian, French, and English. The American edition is under the auspices of the Graymoor Friars, founded by Father Paul. The French edition is in the hands of the Assumption Fathers, who perpetuate the "Church Unity" tradition.

Unitas undertakes the task of spreading information. This review keeps its readers up-to-date on current facts and events of modern ecumenism. Admittedly, the somewhat apologetic tone of some of its contents does little to promote rapprochement with Protestantism. Nevertheless, those who devote themselves to the task of initiating Catholics to the problems of Christian unity should be recognized and encouraged for their thankless job.

Centers of theological influence are more important in the formation of ecumenical thought. Abbé Couturier was primarily concerned with piety. He was right. Yet he did not want to discourage theologians who tackle the great historical and doctrinal problems that divide Christians. He simply felt that spiritual rapprochements were more efficacious at the time. Only later, when there is a meeting of hearts, can the unavoidable theological debate be started. We cannot achieve an intelligent understanding without first being united in mutual friendship.

It is also necessary to state that the doctrinal dialogue between theologians orientated to ecumenism cannot be undertaken too speedily, which is a point that Abbé Couturier possibly did not take sufficient account of. Christian rapprochement on the level of ideas is a long-range task. And we should not await an intimate union of hearts to take up theological discussions. These even seem indispensable to the development of a true brotherhood among separated Christians. No one can love a man whom he does not know. Theological dialogue is the only means capable of providing knowledge of doctrines as these are understood by Christians separated from us. Couturier himself organized theological meetings, as we have seen.

Some of the best known theologians have given tremendous help to the development of a theology of ecumenism. Father Yves Congar wrote the first in a series of theological works on ecumenism, called *Separated Christians* (1937). The *Unam Sanctam* collection has made a specialty of this. The Dominicans have taken a lead in this area. Near Paris Father C. J. Dumont directs the *Istina* center of studies, which is mainly concerned with Russian Orthodoxy, but takes in all ecumenical problems. Its quarterly publication *Istina* and its monthly bulletin *Vers l'unité chrétienne* are invaluable means of information and theological formation. The *St. Irenaeus Center* has been established at Lyons very recently. Here some of Father Dumont's colleagues are engaged in ecumenical dialogues with Protestantism.

The Benedictine Priory of Chevetogne, transferred from Amay in 1939, is still an important ecumenical center. Dom Clement Lialine (1901-1958), who directed the *Irenikon* review for a long time, gave it a distinctly theological and intellectual orientation.

Apart from established centers, independent theologians who are actively interested in ecumenism should be mentioned. Almost all the theologians in France, Belgium and French-speaking Switzerland could be listed, inasmuch as the majority of them have studied one aspect or other of ecumenism. In a number of books dealing explicitly with the ecumenical movement,[13] numerous studies of Protestantism,[14] Anglicanism,[15] or Orthodoxy [16] have been made. Moreover,

---

[13] See above, p. viii.

[14] For example, Henri Bouillard, *Karl Barth,* 3 vol., 1957; Louis Bouyer, *Du Protestantisme à l'Eglise,* 1954.

[15] For example, Maurice Nedoncelle, *Trois Aspects du Problème Anglo-Catholique au XVIIe siècle,* 1951; Albert Gratieux, *L'Amitié au Service de l'Union,* 1950; Stanislas Cwiertniak, *La Vierge Marie dans la Tradition Anglicane,* 1958.

[16] For example, Albert Gratieux, *A. S. Khomiakov et le Mouvement Slavophile,* 2 vol., 1939; *Le Mouvement Slavophile à la Vielle de la Révolution,* 1953.

some patristic studies are clearly of ecumenical importance. True ecumenism implies a return to sources.

On the whole, then, contemporary French theology has supplied a vast selection of titles on Catholic ecumenism.[17] The work of theologians is on par with that of prophets like Abbé Couturier. They support one another in the construction of a solid doctrinal and spiritual framework. Thanks to them, Catholic ecumenism can march on through the night of separations towards the dawn of full Christian unity.

The convergence of ecumenical thought in Germany and in France is worth mention. On the spiritual level the activity of Max Metzger and Paul Couturier converge. Here and there we find the same insights and the same prophetic views. On the doctrinal level German and French theology join hands in a similar ecumenical endeavor, after having sometimes followed different methods. This meeting constitutes a guarantee of the doctrinal maturity of Catholic ecumenism.

This convergence is now an established fact. A "Catholic conference for ecumenical questions" was founded in 1952. Most of the theologians are from German, Dutch and French-speaking countries. It represents a very significant development of Catholic endeavors toward ecumenism.

---

[17] The bibliography prepared by Abbé Michalon may be referred to: *Eléments de bibliographie sur l'oecuménisme,* 1958.

CHAPTER XIV

THE ANGLO-SAXON APPROACH

*"Only the grace of God and the working of the Holy
Spirit can create unity of faith."*
—Henry St. John

The formation of Catholic ecumenism requires a slow matu-
ration. Prophetic voices within the Church are not enough.
A concourse of external circumstances which force Catholics
to look towards "the others" is needed. In the last analysis,
only the Holy Spirit raises true prophets. And circumstances
that influence the direction that the Church takes are themselves providential. Men can resist the Spirit. Oftentimes they
unconsciously oppose with their formidable inertia the in-
distinct desires for renewal that pervade the Church from
time to time. Only he who has never resisted grace has the
right to throw the first stone. No one should be surprised then,
if a prophetic movement like Catholic ecumenism has not
progressed everywhere at a like speed. Germany, Holland,
Belgium, Switzerland and France are in the lead. The hierarchy has the obligation to try spirits before approving them.
Leo XIII deliberately opened the door to ecumenism. De-

pending on conditions at the time, Benedict XV and Pius XI
had encouraged or tempered the movement. Above all, the
popes and the bishops of the countries concerned have had the
foresight to introduce ecumenism into official Church policy
in respect to Christian groups that are separated from her.

Ecumenical thought has not always followed the same path
everywhere, however. In France as well as in Germany, not
everybody concerned with the problems of Christian reunion
shared the position of Max Metzger or Paul Couturier. There
was still what you might call a delayed pre-ecumenism here
and there. This uneven march of ecumenism is even more
pronounced when we turn our attention from German or
French theology to English-speaking theology. Here there
is a truly different situation than that which we have discussed
up till now. Neither great charismatic voices nor world-
renowned theologians dominate. Henceforth there is no un-
definable halo like that surrounding the figure of Max Metzger,
the martyr for peace, or of Abbé Couturier. Catholic ecumenism nevertheless has its pioneers in England and America.
The problems are not those of Germany or France. Yet
Anglo-Saxon Catholicism is shrewd enough to realize that
problems exist, and studies offering solutions are lacking
neither in originality nor in breadth.

Newman's country, England, would seem to be the choice
spot for Catholic ecumenism. It has the advantage of being
the home of Anglicanism, the country where sixteenth century
Reformation is least removed from the Catholic Church.
Following up the Oxford Movement, the Anglo-Catholic
Movement has restored a number of Catholic beliefs and
practices. It has tried to make Catholicism, even Roman
Catholicism, more meaningful to Anglicans. And there have
been ecumenical events in the history of English Catholicism.
Newman's career in the past century was one of them. New-
man wanted to fill the void that separates Catholicism and
Protestantism. He did this in his "Conferences on Justifica-
tion" (1838), written while he was still an Anglican. Some

time later he studied the problems of Anglicanism in his conferences on "Certain Anglican Difficulties" (1850) and in the two volumes of "The *Via Media* of the Anglican Church" (1877). This was a valuable contribution, but it was not enough to forge a movement of opinion.

After Newman, Baron von Hügel (1852-1925) kept the torch of early Catholic ecumenism burning. His spiritual works were appreciated outside Catholicism as well as within. Many Protestant Christians were pleased to call him an "evangelical" soul who was above denominational quarrels.

The baron's letters to his niece are a model of ecumenical correspondence. The baron was a Catholic. His Anglican niece had often consulted him on matters pertaining to her interior life. Spiritual direction of an Anglican by a Catholic is a delicate matter, but in a case where it is necessary and where the Catholic is competent, there is no reason why it should be denied. Von Hügel possessed a rare finesse in these matters. The tact with which he performed his task might well serve as a model for many directors of conscience. His principle was to respect his niece's Anglicanism. "On careful examination," he wrote her, "I saw that I had no even direct intention of attracting you to Rome through your spiritual reading. I simply wanted to give you the best, the strongest food for your soul." [1] He asked her to take the following advice, that has a truly ecumenical spirit: "Do your very best where you are, with what you can get there, taking care only not to fix yourself up negatively, I mean against Roman Catholicism." [2]

Von Hügel made a laudable effort to keep up relations with some modernists in order to keep them from going too far. He knew Alfred Loisy (1857-1940) and the Englishman George Tyrell (1861-1909), who died fortified with the sacraments of the Church and who had apparently kept the

---

[1] Gwendolyn Greene, *Letters from Baron von Hügel to a Niece,* 1928, p. 116.
[2] *Ibid.,* p. 115.

Catholic faith. He maintained contact with them without taking part in the intellectual revolt of the first or the violence of the second. But the modernist crisis had enflamed men's minds. It made it impossible to develop ecumenical thought outside the small circle of Von Hügel's close friends.

After the First World War the Malines Conversations were of immediate interest to England. Anglican participants attended them. Their Catholic partners were still Belgians and Frenchmen. In England itself there were some Catholics who were happy over the Conversations. Lord Halifax had even wanted to bring along an English Jesuit who was of a truly irenic spirit, Father Leslie Walker. Unfortunately, Abbé Portal had very little confidence in the Society of Jesus, and Cardinal Mercier preferred not to be associated with one of its members, at least not in these circumstances. Father Walker held no malice against them, however. He wrote articles that were favorable to the Conversations.[3] He would have been qualified to hold an honorable place in them. It is a pity that he was overlooked, inasmuch as he was sympathetic to the cause. The presence of an English Catholic might possibly have calmed the polemics that eventually exploded.

But even if Cardinal Mercier had been well disposed towards having Father Walker, others would not have been satisfied. Cardinal Francis Bourne (1861-1935), Archbishop of Westminster, had an easily understandable objection. He had been informed of the Conversations, but he would also have liked to follow each step in their course, as the Archbishop of Canterbury did. And he would have wished to send some Englishmen to Malines. It was evidently not good diplomacy to deal with English Anglicans and Protestants as if English Catholics did not even exist. The organizers of the Malines Conversations were not the only ones who adopted this attitude, without thinking anything of it. It would seem that, during his visit to England, Abbé Couturier carefully avoided

---

[3] *Anglia quaerens fidem*, in *Gregorianum*, 1922, vol. 3, pp. 219-38; 337-54.

English Roman Catholics.[4] Is it surprising, then, that the English Catholic hierarchy thought this rather strange? Be that as it may, a troublesome episode cast a shadow over the Malines Conversations in 1925 and '26. Father Woodlock, an English Jesuit, published a violent attack against Cardinal Mercier. He bluntly accused the Belgian cardinal of putting Catholicism in danger. Father Woodlock was poorly informed, incompetent, and uncivil. But many agreed with the substance of what he said.

In spite of these hindrances, Catholic ecumenism reappeared in England during these same years. It began making itself known through some periodicals. *Blackfriars,* published by the Dominicans at Oxford, had some editors who were interested in Anglicanism and Protestantism. Father Vincent McNabb (1868-1943), well known as a public speaker in Hyde Park, often wrote on the separated Churches. He was not a champion of ecumenism, but he wrote in a sympathetic and understanding manner.[5] Father Henry St. John, himself a convert from Anglicanism, also wrote, as he still does, for *Blackfriars.* He has not only written on Anglicanism and Protestantism but on ecumenism as such.[6]

This does not compare very well with ecumenism on the continent. It puts too much emphasis on what separates and on the difficulties of dialogue. But as a whole it is going in the right direction, with the possibly necessary delay that is due to a predominant desire to be realistic and to the fear of inspiring separated Christians with false hopes. It somewhat lacks the spiritual dimension that Abbé Couturier held so important. Preoccupation with doctrine, necessary as it is, does not always inspire a desire to reach hearts. Thus Father St. John writes: "God alone can cause the truth to emerge, because unity in faith is His gift. But we may believe that He will give it in His own time to those who long for it, pray

---

[4] Maurice Villain, *L'abbé Paul Couturier,* p. 122.
[5] Vincent McNabb, *The Church and Reunion,* 1937.
[6] See Henry St. John, *Essays in Christian Unity,* 1955.

for it and will work for it." [7] This may suggest that since Catholics already have unity of faith, they have no need of developing ecumenism through desire, prayer, and work. This is still a stage of pre-ecumenism.

The final step is made when we come to the work being undertaken by the Benedictine quarterly review, *The Eastern Churches Quarterly*.

In 1913, with the exception of a few members, the community of an Anglican Benedictine Abbey situated on the Isle of Caldey off the coast of Wales passed over to Catholicism.[8] The monks who remained Anglicans founded Nashdom Abbey which is flourishing today. Most of the others were received into the Order of St. Benedict by Dom Columba Marmion. They later transferred their monastery to Prinknash. Prinknash Abbey has not forgotten its Anglican origins. Its bulletin, *Pax,* used to have a supplement devoted to Church unity that primarily gave news about the Eastern Churches. Just as has happened elsewhere, it was easier to interest Catholics of a nation that was mainly Anglican in separated Christians who were far off than in their own neighbors. It is occasionally necessary to use this means to arouse interest in the ecumenical problem. Regardless, the *Pax* supplement was discontinued in 1935. It became *The Eastern Churches Quarterly,* directed by the late Dom Bede Winslow, of St. Augustine's Abbey, Ramsgate.

Dom Bede Winslow must be considered the pioneer of Catholic ecumenism in Great Britain. He directed the review from the beginning. He likewise widened its scope by including Anglicanism. Dom Bede gathered some laymen around him in study circles. Betwen 1944 and 1948 he also organized an annual gathering at Oxford. Dom Bede's interpretation was on a parallel with those of Max Metzger and Abbé Couturier. He tried to establish a friendly dialogue,

[7] *Essays in Christian Unity,* p. 72.
[8] See the biography of the founder of Caldey: *Abbot Extraordinary, a memoir of Aelred Carlyle, 1874-1955,* by Peter Anson, 1958.

mainly with Orthodoxy and Anglo-Catholicism. For this
end he spread a sympathetic understanding of the Orthodox
Churches and their theology. This naturally leads to posing
the ecumenical question in its broadest sense, namely, the
rapprochement of Christian communities through mutual
love and understanding.

The Second World War was an occasion for rapprochement
among English Christians. On December 10, 1939, two
months after the outbreak of hostilities, Cardinal Hinsley
(1865-1943), the Archbishop of Westminster, launched an
appeal to the British nation. He asked that the war with
Germany be not simply a test of military force. He hoped
that it would also inspire an interior renewal in men through
a struggle against all forms of moral evil. A few months later
Cardinal Hinsley founded a movement called "The Sword
of the Spirit." Its stated purpose was "the union of all
Christians in a crusade for the restoration of order, justice,
and peace." Catholics could become full members, and other
Christians could become associate members. The success of
the movement during the war years was astonishing. It accomplished an enormous amount of practical work by way
of mutual spiritual assistance and moral education, particularly among the armed forces. The Archbishop of Westminster
had realized a practical ecumenism on the level of Catholic
action. It had nothing to do with organizing exchanges of
theological viewpoints. It was concerned solely with collabo-
rating with all Christians of good will for the spiritual transformation of society on the occasion of a national crisis.

A movement of this sort depends largely on the political
and social data that influence the crisis in which it originates.
The Archbishops of Canterbury, first Cosmo Gordon Lang
(1864-1945), then his successor William Temple (1882-
1944), responded generously to the cardinal's appeal. All
during the War, practical collaboration was the order of the
day, except for some dioceses whose bishops did not share
the methods of the Archbishop of Westminster. The death

of Cardinal Hinsley, then of William Temple, slowed down the movement. With the end of the War, tempers returned to "normal." The "Sword of the Spirit" lost its character as a movement for the fraternity of all Christians. It presently exists as an organization interested in social questions.

An event, ordinary in itself, happened in 1949 which showed that ecumenical endeavours were very much alive in the minds of Catholics. On October 31st a correspondent of the London *Times* published an article on Catholicism. It was followed by an exchange of letters in the *Times* columns that lasted until November 29th. The article itself was nothing sensational, but the correspondence showed that Catholics had ecumenical desires.[9] Dom Columba Cary-Elwes wrote that "we Catholics are conscious of the past errors of the Church, of conduct, not of doctrine, and of its human limitations. It (the reunion) will be realized only by a study that goes beyond polemics, that goes more deeply than a controversy on any one particular point. The break was due to something very profound, a lack of love; those who were separated no longer liked the papacy. In certain respects it had become something that could no longer inspire love. Therefore the return will be brought about by means of love, and love blossoms in obedience." [10]

These anxieties also show up in a literature that is in its formative stage. After Vincent McNabb and Henry St. John there were others who explored ecumenism. Dom Columba Cary-Elwes published *The Sheepfold and the Shepherd* (1955), dedicated to "those who seek the unity of Christ in love and in truth." It was a presentation of the Catholic Church written in a "conciliatory spirit" though with a clearly apologetic method. Ecumenism was finally taken up directly

---

[9] These letters have been published in a brochure called *Catholicism today. Letters to the editor reprinted from 'The Times,'* 1949. Some extracts have appeared in *La Documentation Catholique*, 1950, n. 1062, col. 200-210.

[10] D.C., *ibid.*, col. 207.

by John Todd. His book *Catholicism and the Ecumenical Movement* (1956) is an invitation to ecumenism. This author then began an irenic study of Protestantism by writing a book on the founder of Methodism called *John Wesley and the Catholic Church* (1958).

In summary, Catholic ecumenism is gaining ground in Great Britain. While it has not yet reached the mark attained by similar movements on the European continent, it shows great promise for the future.

American Catholics have not yet gone too far in the direction of ecumenism. American Protestantism, being predominantly liberal, is not doctrinal in character, and this does not encourage theological discussion. The "fundamentalist" section of U.S. Protestantism still keeps a firm hold on doctrine, but it is also still actively opposed to anything that smacks of Catholicism. There is not much of a chance here of creating the atmosphere of mutual confidence which is more or less necessary to the development of ecumenical thought. Without it, attempts at rapprochement among separated Christians seem to be a gamble. American society, moreover, does not lend itself to spiritual rapprochements; for no measurable sociological phenomena would correspond to these. The problems that exist throughout a large continent are readily convertible into statistical data. This facilitates the classification of questions and the organization of solutions. It does not make a qualitative understanding of mentalities and an appreciation of differences any easier.

The development of a fully mature ecumenism is therefore naturally impeded by the spirit of competition in American society, where spiritual movements are of hardly sufficient value to make it possible to classify them numerically. Yet beginnings have been made, and they will make it possible for a true ecumenism to blossom later on.

The pre-ecumenism of Paul Wattson's Octave of Prayer and the rather timid ecumenism of the *Unitas* review have acquired a right to status in the United States. The Feeney affair, which happened in Boston in 1949, provided an occasion to reaffirm the official position relative to the question of the salvation of separated Christians. Father Leonard Feeney taught that they are necessarily damned. This doctrine caused Cardinal Richard Cushing, Archbishop of Boston, to intervene. A letter from the Holy Office dated August 9, 1949, then clarified the meaning of the principle that "outside the Church there is no salvation." Without doubt, this is not yet ecumenism. But it clarifies a preliminary question without which there would be no Catholic ecumenism.

Otherwise, concern over relations between religion and society is very marked in American society, which frequently seeks to redefine itself. This immediately brings up the question of relations between Catholicism and religious pluralism in the United States. This is a point of contact with ecumenical thought. Through this means American Catholicism as a whole will be capable of lending itself to ecumenism. The problem was already brought up in these terms in the past century. The American bishops had then taken it up without hesitation. Circumstances bring the question up periodically. Americans are vitally concerned over the problem of the relation between Church and State and mutual relations between Churches.[11]

It is not mere conjecture to think that this urges American Catholicism towards rapprochement with separated Christians. The American theologian, who seems to be most listened to in matters of ecumenism, usually takes up the question from that angle. Father Gustave Weigel has made ecumenism known among Catholics more than anybody else.[12] He also fights a campaign for an understanding of American pluralism. The two problems are related. It would hardly seem realistic to present the ecumenical question in the

---

[11] See John Cogley (ed.), *Religion in America: original essays on religion in a free society,* 1958.

[12] See Gustave Weigel, *A Catholic Primer on the Ecumenical Movement,* 1957; *Faith and Understanding in America,* 1959.

United States on a purely spiritual level, as Paul Couturier did, or on a purely doctrinal level. It must also be put on the sociological level. Father Edward Duff was aware of this, when he published a valuable study on the social thought of the World Council of Churches.[13]

It is still too early to forecast what form American ecumenism will take,[14] but it has already borne results. In 1954 Cardinal Samuel Stritch, Archbishop of Chicago, forbade the presence of Catholic observers at the Evanston Assembly of the World Council of Churches. The Cardinal nevertheless invited Catholics and other Christians to collaborate in social matters. "In our country," he wrote, "there obtain a variety of religious beliefs. In this condition and in these circumstances we shall live together in charity and, while we shall not sacrifice one iota of our faith taught us by Holy Mother Church, we shall collaborate earnestly and honestly with our fellow-citizens against godlessness in public and social life, against the aggressions and encroachments of those evils which are attacking the very foundations of our democracy. To all men of good will we issue the invitation to join with us and to work with us, even with the limitations which obtain, for that measure of good which is possible for us to secure." [15] The American hierarchy did not stop with this appeal for civic collaboration, because in 1958 the Archbishop of Cleveland authorized the presence of two priests at the meeting of the American division of the "Faith and Order" Commission at Oberlin.[16]

Besides this, some exchanges of correspondence ought to be mentioned. These published letters do not represent directly ecumenical thought, but they show that the American Catholic hierarchy is disposed to respond sympathetically

---

[13] *The Social Thought of the World Council of Churches*, 1956.
[14] Tavard, *The Church, the Layman and the Modern World*, 1959.
[15] Pastoral letter of June 29, 1954.
[16] These priests were Father Gustave Weigel and Father John Sheerin, editor of the monthly publication *The Catholic World*.

to attempts at rapprochement that have in mind an exchange of information.

Between October 19, 1945, and April 12, 1957, the Reverend Dick Hall, a Southern Baptist minister and Archbishop Gerald O'Hara, Archbishop of Savannah, Georgia, an apostolic delegate to London, exchanged long letters. In his letter dated November 28, 1955, the Archbishop explains Catholic doctrine in response to the Baptist pastor's questions, which were very elementary, to tell the truth. In this letter Archbishop O'Hara emphasized: "I will be happy to know that it was possible for us to proceed with an exchange of information with courtesy and understanding."

In 1954, on the occasion of the ninth centenary of the Eastern schism, the Greek Orthodox Bishop in Los Angeles, Bishop Athenagoras Kokkinakis, Bishop of Elaia, and Cardinal McIntyre, Archbishop of Los Angeles, also undertook a dialogue by correspondence. It was started by Bishop Athenagoras. His two long letters and the Cardinal's answers are models of true courtesy.

In his letter of July 9th the Cardinal said: "We honor our Orthodox brethren for their constancy in the apostolic faith in the midst of the greatest difficulties. We Catholics always preserve the hope of a perfect union in this faith." [17]

This new American ecumenism feels somewhat reserved towards the more highly developed forms of Catholic ecumenism in Germany or France. It fears that Europeans are not well informed on the American situation. A Church-wide ecumenism should understand that American Protestantism dominates the Protestant world by sheer strength of its numbers as well as by its financial possibilities and its missionary spirit. But American Protestantism, which is more activist than doctrinal, hardly seems capable today of under-

[17] See *Istina*, 1955, pp. 434-439 (incomplete text); the correspondence has been published in English and Greek under the title *Contemporary Western Orthodox and Roman Catholic Communications*, 1957. The quotation is found on p. 10.

standing, or even believing in, the sincerity of the spiritual
and doctrinal ecumenism of European Catholic theologians.
Ecumenism has to be adapted to the conditions obtaining in
each country. It is conceivable that it take diverse forms.
Americans tend to think that European Catholic ecumenism
is not realistic enough.

Such a down-to-earth reminder must not be disregarded.
Some overly-human frictions hinder a spiritual fellowship of
minds and thereby keep rival Christian communions apart.
We must learn to take account of these clashes in our attitudes. But American Catholics should not forget that
Protestantism itself is growing and changing. American Protestantism, like that of Europe, will gain depth by a return
to the sources which ecumenism should produce. As matters
stand, the proper function of Catholic ecumenism is precisely
to assist such a return to the sources of the Gospel.[18]

Appendix

A special treatment of ecumenism in Italy and Spain does not
fit into this study because Protestant and Orthodox Christians
are a minority in these countries. They are aware of ecumenism,
however.

As for Spain, we may mention the two large volumes entitled
El Movimiento Ecumenista (1953), which contain respectively
the papers given at the 12th Spanish week of theology (Sept.
17-22, 1952), and the 13th week of biblical studies (Sept. 24-29,
1952). One should also be familiar with *Catolicismo y Protestantismo como Formas de Existencia*, 1952, and *El Protestantismo y la Moral*, 1954, both by José Luis Aranguren. Many of
Aranguren's ideas are debatable, but these books show a profound and understanding study of Protestantism. Jorge Tzebrikov
de Villardo has also written a study on Orthodoxy, *El Espiritu
del Cristianismo Ruso*, 1954.

Books on ecumenism are on the increase in Italy, for example,
I Fratelli separati e noi (1941) by Paolo Manni, *Crisi Protes-*

---

[18] On the subject of ecumenism in Europe and America, refer to
the dialogue between Dom Thomas Sartory and Father Gustave
Weigel; *Una Sancta*, 1958, pp. 162-5 and 293-4.

tante e Unità della Chiesa (1939) by Igino Giordani, *Cattolicesimo ed Ecumenismo* (1957) by Edmond Chavaz, and *Il Protestantesimo ieri ed oggi* (1958), edited by A. Piolanti.

We should also be aware that a movement towards Catholic-Orthodox friendship that fosters a truly ecumenical spirit is being promoted in the Lebanon by the Missionaries of St. Paul. Since January, 1956, a quarterly called *Bulletin de Orientation Oecuméniques* has been published at Beyrouth.

CHAPTER XV

17 ROUTE DE MALAGNOU

"Radical changes in thought and structure will have to take place before our Churches will again be truly responsive to the divine call."

—Dr. Visser't Hooft

The First Assembly of the World Council of Churches met at Amsterdam from August 22 to September 4, 1948. It had been "in process of formation" ever since "Life and Work" at Oxford and "Faith and Order" at Edinburgh decided to unite. Among Protestants the ecumenical movement had made great progress since 1937. Instead of being divided into two groups, both striving towards unity but in different ways, one through doctrine and the other through action, it became a single movement that preserved the traditions of its constituent sources. Instead of remaining an association of individuals who were undoubtedly representative, yet acting on their own, it became a single association of group organizations, namely, of Churches.

The formation of the World Council marked a big step forward in the cause of Christian unity. From now on the

member Churches would recognize that the problem of unity
and reunion is organic. There would always be room for
prophets and pioneers, but henceforth they would operate
within the framework of a group rapprochement between
denominations. The Council does not put an end to separations, nevertheless it encourages every rapprochement im-
aginable. It forces the member Churches to come together,
if only at the Council itself. This is all the more important
as the Catholic Church herself is gradually taking up the
question of Christian reunion on the collective level. The
existence of the World Council is therefore one of those
facts that modify the very structures of the world in which
the Church lives, and which at least calls for a re-examination,
not of doctrines, but of problems.

The Amsterdam Assembly was the largest of the ecumenical conferences.[1] The program of discussions there is quite
impressive. The general theme of the Assembly, entitled
"Human disorder and God's Design" was distributed among
four sections. The theme was divided into the following four
parts:

(1) The Universal Church in God's Design.
(2) The Church's Witness to God's Design.
(3) The Church and the Disorder of Society.
(4) The Church and International Disorder.

Books had been prepared on these subjects. They had been
put into the hands of the participants in advance and were to
be published shortly after the close of the Assembly. Altogether these four volumes make up a valuable series for
appraising the development of ecumenical thought at Amsterdam. It should be readily observed that the four divisions
of the general theme follow closely along the same lines as
the two older movements "Faith and Order" and "Life and

---

[1] See Dr. W. Visser't Hooft (ed.), *The First Assembly of the
World Council of Churches. Official Report*, 1949.

Work." The first two sections took up doctrinal questions on
the nature of the Church. The other two took up the practical
applications that "Life and Work" had made its specialty.

In addition to these four sub-topics, the Assembly discussed the reports of four committees, which were occupied
respectively with the following questions:

(1) The constitution of the World Council.
(2) The "politics," i.e., the nature and end of the Council.
(3) The administration of the World Council.
(4) The problems of the Churches.

The problems of the Churches were evidently numerous.
A choice had to be made, and four topics were selected:

(1) The life and function of women in the Church.
(2) The significance of the laity in the Church.
(3) The Christian attitude towards Jews.
(4) Mutual aid and reconstruction after the destructions
    of the War.

The first three committees occupied themselves with relatively new questions raised by the formation of the World
Council. The fourth continued the discussions formerly taken
up by "Faith and Order" and "Life and Work."

The Amsterdam Assembly immediately indicated what the
World Council would be. Born of previous ecumenical groups
and a missionary movement, it was to be more than a simple
union of two organizations. The fundamental themes and the
problems of the fourth committee are discussed *on the Church
level*. Neither the Amsterdam Assembly nor the World Council established there form a Church as such. But it is not
enough to think in terms of denominations. One should also
reflect, meditate, discuss, and pray in terms of the unity willed
by Christ, that is, in terms of the Church. In order to understand the Amsterdam documents, indeed, to understand the

entire contemporary Protestant ecumenical movement, the
dialectic of the one and the many, of unity and divisions, of
the Church and Churches must all be taken into account. This
dialectic provides the framework in which the entire thought
of the World Council of Churches, which is a concrete realization of unity in diversity, develops. The Church, as God
wills it to be in Jesus Christ, is perfectly one. The Churches
are historically divided. The purpose of the World Council
and the sole reason for its existence is to help the Churches
rediscover the Church and, if possible, to help the Church
penetrate the Churches and make them one. The centrifugal
concept of "unity," or "the Church" has been identified with
Christology. The unity that is sought, and which is already
the object of faith, is not a unity of administration, although
there will eventually have to be a single administration. Nor
is it unity of belief or of a common doctrine, even though it
implies such a unity. The unity that is sought is none other
than the divine act by which God communicates Himself in
Christ to His Church. It is a divine gift that the Savior has
guaranteed us. It cannot therefore be the prerogative of the
Council. By virtue of its constitution, the member-Churches
officially profess their faith in Our Lord Jesus Christ, God
and Savior. This was the very same formula that the American Episcopal Church, inspired by Charles Brent, proposed
on October 19, 1910. This Christological formula, entirely
faithful to the Council of Chalcedon, which defined Catholic
orthodoxy against the Monophysite and Nestorian heresies,
puts faith in Christ at the center of all World Council interests. The dialectic of the Church and the Churches revolves
around one common point, faith in the Lord Jesus Christ.
Faith plays the role of catalyst between the Church as object
of faith and the Churches that are historically divided. Now
we must ask ourselves in what sense the word "faith" is to be
taken, because Catholics and Protestants oftentimes apply
different connotations to the word.

The meaning of faith that the World Council has at heart is well described in the "message to the Churches" adopted by the Amsterdam Assembly. This faith is more a consecration than a belief. "Our gathering together in a World Council would be useless if Christians and Christian communities everywhere did not consecrate themselves to the Lord of the Church in a fresh effort to strive together, wherever they are, to be His witnesses and His servants." The words used for this consecration of oneself are those which God repeats to the Church yesterday, today, and tomorrow. "It is because the world is in the hands of the living God, whose will is perfectly good; it is because in Jesus Christ His incarnate Son, who lived, died, and rose from the dead God has once and for all conquered the power of evil and opened up to all the gates of liberty and joy in the Holy Spirit. It is because the final judgment of human history and of all human acts is a judgment made by the merciful Christ, and because the end of history will be the triumph of His reign, where we will at last understand how much God has loved the world." In consecrating itself by these words, the Church knows how to say "yes" and "no," "to say 'no' to all that offends Christ's love, and 'yes' to all that is in keeping with the love of Christ." Thus the Council attempts to balance the Catholic insistence on the object of faith, and the Protestant insistence on the subjective value of faith. The latter is predominant, however. Faith is at once repentance and hope, witness and love. It no doubt implies beliefs, but the Council itself does not define them. It is not a Church and therefore cannot assume the right to define what the Churches are to believe.

Even before the Amsterdam Assembly and while still in process of formation, the World Council had already made some important moves. All through the War a provisional committee created at Utrecht in 1938 had supported the ideal of the World Council that was being formed. The legislative assembly which was supposed to meet in 1940 or 1941 had to be postponed till 1948. The provisional committee had nevertheless continued functioning as normally as possible while faced with a number of difficulties brought about by the international situation. During the three years immediately following the War, its Commission on Cooperation and Reconstruction was busily at work. Together with the International Missionary Council it created a Commission for International Affairs which did and still does keep a close watch on the United Nations and its affiliated organizations. A Department of Studies has produced significant work, particularly in preparing the Themes of the Assemblies. Finally, an Ecumenical Institute has been established at Bossey, near Geneva, for the purpose of initiating students to ecumenical problems.

All of this continued after Amsterdam, while the organization and nature of a council were being more clearly defined.[2]

The World Council of Churches is directed by a Central Committee made up of a hundred members who act as the official representatives of their Churches. This Committee meets about once a year. Its function is to control and direct everything that goes on under the auspices of the World Council. A very small executive committee meets about every six months. Its function is to apply the decisions of the general assemblies and the Central Committee. But in case of emergency it can also make decisions of which it gives an account at the following session of the Central Committee. In addition to this, a permanent secretary resides at Geneva at 17 Route de Malagnou.

The nature of the World Council of Churches has been defined on various occasions. Since this is something entirely new in the lifetime of Christianity, equivocations must be carefully avoided. Otherwise the entire future of the unity movement may be compromised. For this reason the Central Committee forced itself to guard against any equivocation.

---

[2] See a volume prepared for the Evanston Assembly, *The First Six Years, 1948-54.*

The principal document on this matter is the statement on "the Church, the Churches, and the World Council," published by the Central Committee at its assembly in Toronto in July 1950.[3] This statement formally denies that the ecumenical movement implies "the basic equality of all Christian doctrines and all concepts of the Church." All the traditions represented remain free to define themselves as they wish. All the Churches retain their autonomy and their spiritual responsibility. The Council does not supplant the Churches. It does not interfere with their administration. It does not pretend to be God's one, holy, catholic, apostolic Church, the object of faith. It does not aspire to become a "Super-Church," a kind of federation which would gradually absorb the Churches. The secretary of the World Council, Dr. Visser't Hooft, so deliberately avoids the idea of a "Super-Church" as to have written an article on the subject in 1958.[4] In this article he described the "Super-Church" as an "apocalyptic Babylon," by way of contrast with what the World Council wants to be.

If the Council is not that, then what is it? It is simply a means for keeping the idea of Christian unity before the Churches. "Through its existence and its activities the Council gives evidence of the necessity of showing clearly the unity of Christ's Church." [5] Its very existence encourages the Churches to criticize themselves, at least as regards to Christian divisions. It makes possible the friendly mutual criticism that is spontaneously born of meetings between Christians of divergent traditions.

Then the World Council becomes a corrective element in the life of the Churches. According to the Protestant axiom *ecclesia reformata semper reformanda,* the Church must reform itself even though it is already reformed. It must always

---

[3] French text in *Foi et Vie,* January-February 1951, pp. 73-81.

[4] *The Super-Church and the Ecumenical Movement,* in *The Ecumenical Review,* 1958, pp. 365-85.

[5] *Foi et Vie, ibid.,* p. 75.

remain attentive to the Word. The sixteenth century Reformation was not the last reformation of the Church. The ever-
present task of making Christian life and its framework more
conformed to Christ must be constantly pursued. In this
sense the ecumenical movement strives to be a twentieth
century reformation, issuing from, and where necessary, correcting that of the sixteenth century. *The Renewal of the
Church* by Dr. Visser't Hooft, secretary general of the Council, gives a good insight into this ideal. In this book Dr.
Visser't Hooft shows that the Church is oftentimes "renewed" at the expense of its "unity." But a true renewal must
respect unity. "In the Bible, renewal and unity are not seen
as alternatives or as competing objectives." [6] "Recent ecumenical history has made us understand better that the gift
of renewal, like every spiritual gift, is given 'for the common
good' (I Cor., 12:7), that is for the upbuilding of the whole
body in its unity." [7] The historic Church must reform in the
sense of the unity of the one spiritual Church.

By what means will such a reform take place? By study,
first of all; a study that always goes back to the Christological
foundation of the Council as established at the beginning.
The "Faith and Order" Commission undertakes this study.
Other commissions take the study of evangelism, that is, the
question of how to present the Gospel to the modern world.
Others study missionary problems and relations between the
Church and State. Study has to be joined to action in carrying through with the twentieth century reformation. The
Council has therefore created commissions on youth, on the
cooperation of men and women in the Church, and on the
laity. Besides this, the Commission on International Affairs
and the Division of Inter-Church Aid bring ecumenical work
to all spheres of modern life.

The Commission on Faith and Order held a general as-

---

[6] *The Renewal of the Church*, p. 119.
[7] *Ibid.*, p. 123.

sembly at Lund in 1952 which we have already mentioned. It then decided to introduce liturgical questions among the problems of ecumenism. Its American division organized a local assembly in 1958. It met at Oberlin, Ohio.

The Commission for the Missions is a joint Commission that depends on both the World Council and the International Missionary Council. A search for unity by means of an internal reformation of the Churches has to see the unity of the Church and its evangelical mission together. This mission is none other than the application of the Gospel. It bears witness to unity inasmuch as it essentially consists in making the Church's unity more universal. It is therefore inevitable that the World Council become more and more interested in missionary action. This is of the very nature of the problems at hand.

The Second General Assembly of the World Council of Churches took place at Evanston, near Chicago, August 15-31, 1954.[8] The activities of this congress came under the general heading of "Christ, the hope of the world," [9] and six sub-topics: (1) Faith and Order: Our oneness in Christ and our disunity as Churches.[10] (2) Evangelism: The mission of the Church to those outside her life.[11] (3) Social Questions: The responsible society in a world perspective.[12] (4) International affairs: Christians in the struggle for world community.[13] (5) Intergroup relations: The Churches amid racial and ethnic tensions.[14] (6) The laity: The Christian in his vocation.[15]

----

[8] See Visser't Hooft (ed.), *L'Assemblée d'Evanston*, 1955; Tavard, *L'Assemblée d'Evanston*, in *Lumiere et Vie*, January 1955, pp. 110-116.

[9] Text in *Istina*, 1954, pp. 182-218.

[10] Text in *Istina*, 1954, pp. 352-60.

[11] Text in *Istina*, 1954, pp. 443-52.

[12] Text in *Istina*, 1954, pp. 452-67. See *Ethical Issues at Evanston* in *The Christian Century*, October 30, 1954. This article, written by "a European Roman Catholic," is the work of a German writer.

[13] Text in *Istina*, 1954, pp. 468-86.

[14] Text in *Istina*, 1954, pp. 486-96.

[15] Text in *Istina*, 1954, pp. 497-509.

A statement had been prepared on each of these topics. They were submitted to the Assembly, discussed, amended, and finally were sent to the Churches for whom they were being studied. The Evanston Assembly has been criticized more than that of Amsterdam. Its American hosts have been reproached for the sensational publicity that surrounded the Assembly, the invasion of journalists who, knowing little about ecumenical affairs, had a poor understanding of the purpose of, and methods employed by, the World Council. Having thousands of spectators at some of its meetings turned the theological discussion into a spectacle. And there were a few regrettable frictions with Catholicism. Following the Assembly from a distance, Catholics were astonished at the attacks made against the Church by Santos Barbieri, a Methodist bishop in Argentina. They were even more surprised when Santos Barbieri was elected as one of the presidents of the World Council. Protestants on their side had gotten a bad impression from the pastoral letter of Cardinal Samuel Stritch, who warned Catholics against attending the conference.

Some Catholic theologians had carefully studied the main theme of the Assembly, however. In its April-June issue of 1954 the review *Istina* had published a Catholic study on "Christ, the Church and Grace in the Economy of the Redemption." [16] In the light of Catholic theology it treated the principal topics of the report on "Christ, the hope of the world," and of the report made by Faith and Order on "unity and disunity." An English translation had even been sent to all the delegates. [17]

---

[16] *Istina*, 1954, pp. 132-158.

[17] There are two English translations of this Catholic document. One, published under the auspices of *Istina*, was forwarded to the delegates. Unfortunately it didn't reach all the delegates on time. Two weeks before the Assembly, Dr. Visser't Hooft, in New York at the time, was not aware that a translation had been made. At his request the present author translated the French text into English.

Despite the misgivings that can hardly be avoided at such assemblies, Evanston made a step forward in the march of the ecumenical movement towards a true reformation in the light of the Gospel. The central lesson of the Assembly consists in the fact that the delegates, in the name of the Church, invited the Churches to an examination of conscience.

"As we learn more of our unity in Christ, it becomes the more intolerable that we should be divided. We therefore ask you: Is your Church seriously considering its relation to other Churches in the light of our Lord's prayer that we may be sanctified in the truth and that we may all be one? Is your congregation, in fellowship with sister-congregations around you, doing all it can do to ensure that your neighbours shall hear the voice of the one Shepherd calling all men into the one flock?"

This appeal is based on the theology of the reports presented at Evanston. The Lutheran principle by which every Christian is at once "sinning and justified" was now extended to the entire Church. Catholic theology was due to criticize this.[18] The description of the Christian as "sinning and justified" is true, since there is not even a saint who is not also a sinner. But it is not true of the Church, which, according to St. Paul and all the catholic tradition, is without blemish. Whatever expressions were employed at Evanston, the effort to have the Churches themselves repent of their divisions characterizes the direction ecumenism is taking in its new reformation of the Christian life for achieving a deeper fidelity to the Gospel.

Since the Evanston Assembly the life of the World Council has been characterized above all by the convergence of the increasing missionary enterprises of the Council and the ac-

This translation was mimeographed under the auspices of the World Council and made available to the delegates.

[18] See Tavard, *Un point de vue catholique sur l'ecclésiologie d'Evanston*, in *Foi et Vie*, January 1955, pp. 54-64.

tivities of the World Missionary Council. Missions are not a specialized activity of the Churches. They are the very life of the Church. It is through missions that the Church founded by the Apostles witnesses here below the approach of the end of time and the second coming of Christ on earth. By means of missions it hastens the coming of the day when the glorified Christ will reconcile all things to His Father, thus perfecting the work of creation and redemption. This eschatological character of missions corresponds to the eschatological meaning of the essential unity of the Church. The reconciliation of all things in Heaven and on earth will not result in a new unity that is still to be created. It will take place in the framework of the unity of the one Church. In the eyes of Protestantism, this unity is not visible today. It is nonetheless real. Missions thus constitute an appeal to the world to find grace in the one Church. Missions imply unity and vice-versa. When the missionary movement of the past century regretted Christian divisions, it bore witness to a profound theological truth. Today it is up to the World Council of Churches to draw the necessary conclusions.

These conclusions have taken the form of a project for amalgamation on the part of the World Council and the Missionary Council. At the meeting of the Central Committee in New Haven, Conn., in August, 1957, the Commission for the Missions was in favor of, and the Central Committee forwarded to the Churches, a project for a merger of the two organizations. In January 1958 this project was provisionally approved by the Missionary Council assembled at Accra, Ghana. Definite decisions have to be made by the Missionary Council and by the next assembly of the World Council.[19]

The expansion of the missionary activities of the World Council is but an instance of the growth of the Council's importance. This growth has continued since the Evanston As-

[19] Some of the dangers of this union are discussed in Tavard, *Protestantism,* 1959.

sembly. There are lessons to be learned from this. One of these is the interest which the World Council presents to the Catholic world. There have not yet been any official Catholic observers at the general assemblies, but Father Charles Boyer, who was in Holland for the Amsterdam Assembly, was able to meet a number of delegates. Four priests attended the Faith and Order Assembly held at Lund in 1952, as official visitors.[20] Two were present at Oberlin in 1958.[21] One attended the meeting of the Central Committee at Nyborg in Denmark in August, 1958. The Central Committee's meeting at Rhodes in the Summer of 1959 was also followed by several Catholic priests. In general, the World Council's Department of Studies is in close touch with the Catholic Conference for Ecumenical Questions. This Conference has also prepared a Catholic report on the theme of the next Assembly of the World Council of Churches, "The Kingship of Christ over the Church and the World."

Another sign of the increasing importance of the World Council is the fact that it has aroused the interest of the Patriarch of Moscow. Some delegates of the Orthodox Church in the Soviet Union met with the delegates of the World Council at Utrecht on August 7-9, 1958. While the Russian Church has not joined the World Council, relations between Moscow and Geneva are improving.

Finally, there are material signs of the extent to which the World Council has increased. The headquarters of the general administration at *17 Route de Malagnou* have become too small. A new building is being planned. This building will possibly witness a spread of ecumenism that would be a tremendous asset to the prophetic and reforming function of the movement. Some look at it this way. Others, on the contrary, see it as a mark of success. After the rather impractical encampment on *Route de Malagnou,* ecumenism

---

[20] Msgr. Assarson, Father de Paillerets, Father Gerlach, and Father Peter Doyle.

[21] See ch. XIV, p. 170, n.16.

will become safe and comfortable. Whatever may be the meaning of this new establishment, it must be recognized as a sign that the World Council of Churches will not be a passing event in twentieth century Christian life. Ecumenism is building for the future.

CHAPTER XVI

HOPES

> *"The Church is the pilgrim people of God. . . . There-*
> *fore the nature of the Church is never to be finally*
> *defined in static terms, but only in terms of that to*
> *which it is going."*
>
> —Leslie Newbigin

A world-wide Christian reunion can only be achieved by small steps. The World Council of Churches hopes for a union where no Christian is excluded. The people at 17 Route de Malagnou know that such a union cannot start off with a pre-established plan. Before getting traditions together that have a wide variance, it is wise to establish points of contact between traditions that are relatively close. Many of the pioneers of ecumenism consecrated themselves to this without even waiting for the formation of the World Council. From Church to Church people have sometimes kept up conversations in view of possible reunion in the future. Scanning the countries and Christian denominations engaged in these conversations, we see that the results have varied considerably. In some cases leisurely discussions have lasted

188

for years to arrive sometimes at poor results or even at the conclusion that no union was possible. There is a Church politics just as there is one of nations. As long as there are meetings, even if it is only to talk and say nothing, there is hope of some day getting around to fruitful endeavors where understanding is possible.

All continents and almost all countries have witnessed such conversations. Many of them have borne results. Unions have been effected. We may classify them according to their order of increase into *cooperative work, intercommunions,* and *unions.* Among the latter we must further distinguish, in terms of the kinds of Churches that united, between *homogeneous* unions and *heterogeneous* unions.

Cooperative work continues. It consists in "federations" or "councils" on the national or local level where Protestant and sometimes Orthodox Churches consult and help one another.

The Federation of the Protestant Churches of France, for example, was the first, having started in 1905. In the United States, another country of pioneers, the Federal Council of Churches of Christ was founded in 1908, and in 1948 it became the National Council of Churches of Christ. It took on the work of "expressing the catholic community and unity of the Christian Church." It takes in most of the Protestant and Orthodox Churches of America.

Several countries followed these examples. Germany did it in 1922 with its *Arbeitsgemeinschaft Christlicher Kirchen,* a federation which disappeared under national socialism. The British countries were somewhat slow to take up this movement: Great Britain in 1942, Canada in 1944, New Zealand in 1945, and Australia in 1946. German Christianity was reorganized after the Second World War. It comprises two federations. *EKD (Evangelischen Kirche in Deutschland),* established in July, 1948, includes Lutheran and Calvinist Churches. *VELKD (Vereinigte Evangelischen-Lutherischen*

Kirche Deutschlands), also founded in July, 1948, is made up solely of Lutheran Churches.[1]

In Asia and Africa Church federations are also common.[2] *Intercommunion* agreements are a very questionable element of modern ecumenism. These agreements permit some Churches to give holy communion to each other's members under determined conditions. This kind of getting together seems to be particularly in favor with the Anglican Church. The "Low Church" theology is hungry for it. Thus Anglicanism enjoys a more or less complete intercommunion with the Swedish Lutheran Church since 1920, the Old Catholics since 1931, the Mar-Thomas Church of the Malabar Coast since 1936, the National Polish Church in the United States since 1946, the Philippine Independent Church since 1948, and the Church of South India since 1955.

The principle of these intercommunions is to be found in the "Book of Common Prayer." In order to receive communion the Prayer Book requires previous baptism and confirmation by a bishop. Intercommunion is therefore possible, in principle, with all Churches whose episcopate is recognized by the Anglican Church. Moreover, under certain extraordinary circumstances it is permissible to give communion to Christians who have been baptized but not confirmed. Some Anglican bishops have taken the responsibility for this on the occasion of ecumenical assemblies. But it is difficult to see where to stop once the principle of intercommunion without doctrinal unity has been admitted.

Unions between Churches have come about more often than intercommunions. *Homogeneous* unions between Lutheran synods were frequent in the United States during the nineteenth century, and they continue. Four American Lutheran Churches are preparing for a union that is to take place in the near future. In France four Protestant Churches formed the Reformed Church of France in 1938. Between

---

[1] See J. P. Michael, *Christen suchen eine Kirche,* 1958, pp. 74-91.
[2] Stephen Neill, *Towards Church Union,* 1952.

1937 and 1952 unions between Lutherans, Calvinists and Methodists were put successfully under way in the United States, Switzerland, Holland, Brazil, and Madagascar. In each case they were the result of conversations that had been carried on for years, even decades. But the result, the union attained, is worthy of an untiring patience.

Heterogeneous unions are even more remarkable because they group together in a single body Churches that have inherited varying traditions. The oldest dates back to 1817. It was imposed by Frederic Wilhelm III, King of Prussia, who was a Calvinist, on the Lutherans and Calvinists of his kingdom. Similar unions have been effected in Japan, Africa, the United States, India, and the Philippine Islands. The most recent heterogeneous union was signed in 1957 by two American Churches, the Congregationalist and the Evangelical and Reformed Church.

It was through a union of this sort, which is no doubt the strangest and the most highly publicized, that the Church of South India was created in 1957. For the first time in history a section of the Anglican Communion left Anglicanism in order to form a new Church with the Protestants of their area. The Anglican Dioceses of Madras, Travancore, Tinnevelly and Dornakal united with Calvinists and Methodists. Only Lutherans, Baptists, and a "High Church" Anglican group remained outside the Church of South India. The transactions that were completed in 1947 had been in process since 1919. The end result was a mixture of the episcopal tradition of Anglicanism and the liberal Calvinist doctrine of the majority of Protestants of that region. The Church of South India therefore has an episcopal framework. It has no doctrine on the nature of the episcopate. The cardinal point in the form taken by the Church of South India is that it does not claim to be a definitively constituted Church. It is a Church in process of formation. A statement prepared by the Church of South India in view of the Lund Conference said in fact: "The Church of South India confesses that it is not yet the Church in the full sense which the word 'Church' ought to have. It confesses itself to be on the road, and it makes a claim to be on the right road, but it does not pretend to have arrived." [3]

This is a courageous experiment. The Church of South India is the result of a profound ecumenical experience. Christians must be led to unity by an act of faith. Those who are thus united have, by suppressing institutional obstacles first of all, thereby desired to give the Spirit the opportunity to guide them more freely towards unity. The Church of South India must be understood in this spirit; it is a witness.

It is easy to criticize the Church of South India. In a sense it has put the cart before the horse because it has preferred administrative union to doctrinal unity. To Catholicism, this is a strategic error. The Lutherans who refused to join the union and the minority who kept their Anglican identity were right in detecting the error of the fundamental principle of the Church of South India.

The idea of participating in an important ecumenical experience is predominant in the Church of South India, however. It is a trial experiment. The plans for union presently in process of preparation in other parts of the world can be judged in the light of this. The mission lands are attracted by its example. Pakistan, North India, Ceylon, and several African regions are contemplating projects that are more or less patterned after that of South India. Its adventurous spirit is contagious. Will it be for the good or the ill of ecumenism? It is still too soon to tell.

One is inclined to think of the Church of England as being very sound and little given to experiments, yet it has felt the disquieting and tempting attraction of union. After the Lambeth Conference of 1888 Anglicanism dreamed of a union of all Churches of the United Kingdom, Anglican and Protestant alike. Conversations were taken up at various times.

---

[3] Leslie Newbigin, *The Household of God,* 1953, p. 25.

From 1832-34, and again from 1949-51, representatives of
the Anglican Church met with delegates of the Scottish Presbyterian Kirk. After they met with a favourable reception to
the statements published after the conversations, both in
Scotland and in England, even larger assemblies were organized from 1955-57 between representatives of four Churches:
the Anglican Churches of England and of Scotland, and the
Presbyterian Churches of Scotland and of England.

A common agreement drawn up in 1957 proposed that
Anglican and Presbyterian ministers recognize one another.
There would be a supplementary ordination of all the clergy.
Anglican priests would receive "imposition of hands" from
the Presbyterians, and the Presbyterian ministers would allow
themselves to be ordained by Anglican bishops. From the
doctrinal point of view the "monarchial" episcopate of the
Anglican Communion was thereby assimilated to the synodal
government of the Presbyterian Churches, the synod having,
according to the proposal, a collective episcopate. In the
event of a union Presbyterians would accept an episcopal
government that would recognize the rights of the synod. It
would be a synodal episcopate presided over by a "Bishop
in presbytery." [4]

In August, 1958, the Lambeth Conference, in the name of
the Anglican bishops, took account of this proposal but
without deciding anything on the subject.[5] In June, 1959, the
General Assembly of the Kirk of Scotland decided against it.
It considered the idea of a synodal episcopate and the proposal of a re-ordination of ministers as "unacceptable in that
they imply a denial of the catholicity of the Church of Scotland and of the validity and regularity of its ministry in the
Church Catholic." [6]

This project therefore died a premature death. The Scottish

---

[4] *Relations between Anglican and Presbyterian Churches. A joint
report*, 1957.
[5] *The Lambeth Conference*, 1958; see the 2nd statement, pp. 40-5.
[6] *Ecumenical Press Service*, June 5, 1959.

Church saw clearly that no fruitful unity could be founded on an ambiguous theology. It is better to remain separated than to unite at the expense of the doctrine that one holds to be true. Charity does not result in unity except in truth.

The many efforts towards rapprochement that we have briefly followed up in this chapter keep the desire for unity alive in a practical way. Thus they merit the understanding attention of all who feel the anxiety of Christian divisions.

Collaborations are oftentimes necessary. *Intercommunions* lead to a dubious sort of theology, but they help the Churches to know one another. *Homogeneous* unions are to be recommended. While they unite Christians having the same doctrine and tradition, they cannot help but be encouraging without being behind the times. *Heterogeneous* unions that unite traditions that are very close to one another are in much the same category. Those that unite the Anglican and Presbyterian traditions, as in South India or as proposed in Great Britain, are the spearhead of contemporary ecumenism. Seen from the viewpoint of theological truth, they must be regarded as dangerous adventures because of the doctrinal ambiguity in which they are enveloped. Nevertheless, in the mysterious designs of Providence they are perhaps the paradoxical means that the Spirit uses to give Protestantism an episcopal structure, the condition *sine qua non* of ultimate reunions.

CHAPTER XVII

BYZANTIUM AND MOSCOW

> *"Holy Tradition taken in its entirety represents the superabundant life of the Ecumenical Church as a living organism, as the Body of Christ living continuously in the Spirit of the Lord."*
> —Sergius, Bishop of Staraya Russa, USSR

The attitude of the Eastern Orthodox towards Church unity has always been very clear from a doctrinal point of view. Church unity is the unity of the Orthodox Churches. But the Orthodox attitude in regard to relations between Christians in the present state of severed Christianity is not so clear.

The history of the past centuries has left its mark on the Orthodox mentality. Relations between Orthodoxy and Protestantism were rare before the twentieth century. There were a few instances. Subsequent to 1573 Lutherans approached Jeremias II, Patriarch of Constantinople (1572-9; 1580-4; 1586-96). It resulted in a respectful but firm invitation to adopt the Orthodox faith. In the following century Patriarch Cyril Lucaris (1672-1738) became notorious for a bold experiment. More for political than for theological reasons, Cyril ventured on a rapprochement with Protestantism. The well-known profession of faith that bears his name is completely Calvinist. It was unfortunate for the unhappy patriarch. He was deposed and reinstated in his see four times and died by strangulation at the order of Sultan Morad. In 1672 a Council held at Jerusalem explicitly condemned Cyril Lucaris' profession of faith. By way of a reaction, a Russian by the name of Peter Moghila (1596-1647) published a catechism inspired by Roman Catholicism and directed the Kiev Academy towards Catholic theology. This again provoked a counter-reaction. Under Theophane Prokopovitch (1681-1736), Bishop of Pskov, Protestant manuals were used for instruction at the Kiev Academy. The theology of Prokopovitch was marked by Calvinism. This coming and going nevertheless did not suffice to establish stable relations with Protestantism.

Relations with Anglicanism were likewise nothing more than sporadic events until the beginning of the twentieth century. The best known incident is the correspondence between the English Non-Jurors and the Eastern Patriarchs and the Holy Synod, which took place between 1716 and 1725. In the nineteenth century, the Oxford Movement, particularly in the case of William Palmer, turned somewhat in the direction of Orthodoxy. There were some Anglicans who traveled to the East. It was more rarely that Orthodox prelates traveled to England. But all this amounted to little.

Orthodoxy has always kept up very consistent relations with Catholicism. There have been periods of peace, even of theological rapprochements, and periods of hostility, depending on circumstances. A lack of mutual understanding is too obvious and a progressive estrangement of mentalities has taken place. Yet there never has been the isolation that for so long a time has separated Orthodoxy and the Churches of the Reformation.

The situation changed towards the end of the nineteenth century. Once again the Anglican bishops undertook an experiment of considerable importance to ecumenism. The

Lambeth Conference of 1888, already celebrated for its definition of the Lambeth Quadrilateral, decided to encourage relations with the Orthodox. It even formulated the purpose of such relations, that is, to prepare for a more complete union between the two Churches by means of exchanges of views and explanations. This was to smooth the way for an organic union with Orthodoxy.

No concrete project was elaborated at the time. On the side of the Orthodox moreover, there was suspicion of the doctrinal discord among Anglicans. In 1902 the Holy Synod stated that an "indispensable" condition was necessary to any union: the entire Anglican Communion and not just its "High Church" party must want union with the Orthodox. At other times Anglican approaches were misunderstood, as though they implied a desire for mass conversion. Thus in 1918 a Russian Council (the last one held before Communism came to power) expressed its pleasure at seeing "the sincere efforts of the Old Catholics and the Anglicans to unite with the Orthodox Church on the basis of the doctrine and tradition of the ancient Catholic Church." [1]

Meanwhile the Old Catholics, having quit the Roman Communion after the definition of papal infallibility, also turned their eyes towards the East. There was a Russian visitor at the first Old Catholic Congress, held in June, 1871. A theological assembly was held at Bonn in September, 1874, for the purpose of bringing about a union of the Old Catholics with the Orthodox. In 1875 a new and more official meeting was held to settle doctrinal and liturgical obstacles. In 1892 a Russian commission decided in favor of the union. But the Old Catholic Congress of 1894 pointed out fundamental differences in the theology of the Trinity on the question of the procession of the Holy Spirit. They kept up their relations just the same, but union was out of the question. The

---

[1] Quoted by George Florovsky in Rouse-Neill, *op. cit.,* p. 213; see *The Anglican and Eastern Churches. A historical record, 1914-21,* 1921.

fact that the Old Catholic Church has turned Protestant in many respects makes any reunion with Orthodoxy a utopian dream.

The Orthodox bishops and theologians paid particular attention to Anglican orders. The East took the condemnation of Anglican orders by Pope Leo XIII in 1896 seriously, and it caused a great deal of commotion there. The Archbishop of Canterbury saw to it that his own response and that of the Archbishop of York were forwarded to a number of Orthodox bishops. Shortly afterwards Cardinal Vaughan sent them the English Catholic bishops' rejoinder to the answer that the Anglicans had made to the Pope.

The Orthodox soon became involved in the theological debate and were no longer mere spectators. Several groups of theologians both in Greece and in Russia set about studying the question in the light of Orthodox canonical and theological tradition. The solutions proposed for the problem of Anglican orders fell into two categories. Following the mind of V. A. Sokolov of the Theological Academy of Moscow and of A. Bulgakov of the Academy of Kiev, the Russian theologians on the whole decided in favor of the validity of Anglican orders.[2] The Greeks came to more subtle conclusions. In the theology of baptism the Russians had previously been more disposed to recognize the validity of the sacrament when administered outside of Orthodoxy. It was the same now with the sacrament of Holy Orders. The most important document of Greek theology on this subject was written by Chrestos Androutsos of the University of Athens, and entitled *The Validity of Anglican Ordinations from the Orthodox-Catholic Point of View* (1899). The point that Androutsos insists on the most is that the question is first of

---

[2] V. A. Sokolov, *One Chapter from an Enquiry into the Hierarchy of the Anglican Episcopal Church,* 1899; A. Bulgakov,. *The Question of Anglican Orders,* 1899. A discussion of the entire question is to be found in Florovsky, *op. cit.,* pp. 209-15. To compare it with the Catholic viewpoint, see F. Clark, *Anglican Orders and Defect of Intention,* 1956.

all not theological but canonical. Theologically, nothing can be concluded with certainty concerning ordinations conferred outside Orthodoxy except that they are performed outside the Church. But canonically speaking, the Church can decide to recognize the validity of the orders of any Anglican priest who wants to join Orthodoxy. The intention of those who ordain or are ordained is doubtful, but the exterior rite of the Ordinal seems to follow the mind of the Church sufficiently in regard to the sacrament of Holy Orders. In effect, therefore, the Church has but to recognize its intention in order to validate the doubtful administration of a sacrament. In such instances Greek theology has recourse to the "principle of economy."

The Orthodox attitude towards Anglican orders can vary, then, depending on how the principle of economy is applied. It has evolved as a matter of fact. In January, 1920, shortly before the world-wide appeal of the Lambeth Conference, the Patriarch of Constantinople addressed a letter "to all the Churches of Christ, wherever they may be." This letter invited the Churches to join together in a common effort even if doctrinal differences prohibited a complete union. Two years later, in July, 1922, the Ecumenical Patriarch forwarded to most of the Orthodox Churches conclusions that were in favor of Anglican ordinations. He thought this would facilitate a collective rapprochement. This favorable judgment of Anglican orders was approved by the Churches of Jerusalem and Cyprus in March, 1923, and by Alexandria in 1930. In 1936 the Church of Roumania cautiously followed suit. It recognized Anglican orders conditionally, asking that the Anglican Churches make an official declaration on the subject of the Eucharist that would be in keeping with the Orthodox faith. The principle of economy would be applied if the Anglican doctrine were judged to be sufficiently Orthodox. In September, 1939, the Greek Church adopted a similar position. While she rejected the essential validity of Anglican orders altogether, she approved a revalidation in particular cases by virtue of the principle of economy.

So there were two positions, one more favorable and the other less favorable to Anglicanism. The latter won out in the end. From July 8-18, 1948, an assembly of Orthodox bishops and theologians met at Moscow to celebrate the fifth centenary of the Autocephalous Russian Church. The Patriarchs of Russia, Roumania, and Yugoslavia were present, and there were official delegations representing all the Orthodox Churches except the Patriarchate of Jerusalem and the Churches of Cyprus and Finland. The representatives of the Ecumenical Patriarchate and of the Greek Church took no part in the theological discussions and did not sign the conclusions. But all the other delegates approved them. At the suggestion of His Beatitude Alexis, Patriarch of Moscow, Anglican orders was one of the subjects discussed. Metropolitan Benjamin, Bishop of Riga and Letonia, declared in his statement that: "Actually there can be no question of recognizing the validity of the sacrament of Holy Orders nor of recognizing apostolic succession in the Anglican Church." [3] By unanimous agreement they declared Anglican orders invalid. They gave as their reason the fact that the Anglican faith is not in agreement with the Orthodox faith. They established as a preliminary condition to their recognition of Anglican Orders an act involving the entire Anglican Church that would show its doctrine on the Eucharist to be in agreement with that of the Orthodox Church. They admitted however, that if Anglicanism were to revise its doctrine on this question it would be possible at some time in the future to revalidate Anglican orders by applying the principle of economy. This condemnation is representative of the present attitude of the Orthodox Churches of Alexandria, Antioch, Russia, Roumania, Bulgaria, Yugoslavia, Poland, and Albania.

---

[3] *Actes de la Conférence des Eglises Autocéphales Orthodoxes*, 2 vol., Moscow, 1950 and 1952; quotation, vol. 2, p. 279.

Due to the fact that the Patriarch of Moscow has regained some influence, Orthodoxy has taken a stiff attitude towards Anglicanism.

Despite its uncompromising stand, Orthodoxy has not given the ecumenical movement the cold shoulder.[4] On the contrary, some of its representatives have taken an active part in all the modern ecumenical assemblies. Ever since the "Faith and Order" and "Life and Work" movements started, their leaders have been in contact with the Orthodox Churches. The delegation of American Anglicans who payed a visit to Benedict XV were also received by the Ecumenical Patriarch. The first result of these contacts was the participation of Orthodox delegates in the Stockholm and Lausanne Assemblies.

There was no dogmatic discussion at the Stockholm Assembly properly so-called. Therefore it was rather easy for the Orthodox and Protestant delegates to get together on a friendly basis. It was a new experience for both sides. Yet one cannot help but get a bad impression of certain press write-ups that spoke of the presence of "Byzantine tiaras" at Stockholm. In the eyes of some Protestants the Orthodox prelates were hardly more than ornaments.

Things were different at Lausanne. This time the Conference dealt with doctrine. The Orthodox bishops and theologians have never hesitated to bear witness to their faith. In the name of all the Orthodox present, Bishop Germanos, the Metropolitan of Thyatire, dissociated himself from most of the statements. The Orthodox voted on nothing apart from the "message to the world." The Metropolitan affirmed the faith of the Orthodox Church: "The union can be effected only on the basis of the common faith and confession of the ancient undivided Church of the seven Councils and of the first eight centuries."[5] He rejected "a concept of reunion

---

[4] See the series of documents ranging from 1902-55 published in *Istina*, 1955, pp. 78-106; 180-214; 389-93.

[5] *Istina*, 1955, p. 104.

that would be reduced to a few points in common expressed in some verbal statements." [6] Ever since the Orthodox first participated in the ecumenical movement they have pointed to the fundamental fault of the method adopted in the great assemblies. Feeling that a state of basic agreement has not been reached, the leaders often strive for an agreement of form and of words for the time being.

The Orthodox delegates went even further. The Bishop of Ochrida, Nicolai Velimirovic, suggested that the Protestants restore the seven sacraments, which are in agreement with the time-honored experience of the saints of the Church.[7] And Sergius Bulgakov, professor at St. Sergius Institute in Paris, contended with the Protestant delegates when he delivered a eulogy to the *Theotokos,* calling her "the head of all men within the Church, the Mother and Spouse of the Lamb." [8]

The Orthodox delegates have therefore profited by the ecumenical assemblies. They have proclaimed at the ecumenical assemblies their willingness to participate in any movement that seriously seeks to reunite Christians. They have also borne witness to their unfailing faith in the doctrinal tradition of Orthodox Christianity, centered on the first seven councils, the seven sacraments, and the Byzantine liturgy.

Thus the Orthodox have continued to take part in the ecumenical movement. In 1937 the World Council for Life and Work published a large volume of Russian Orthodox studies called *Kirche Staatund Mensch.* The Oxford and Edinburgh Assemblies were again honored by the presence of Orthodox delegations. Their attitude had not changed. At Edinburgh the Metropolitan of Thyatire insisted on the "necessity of being exact and concrete in formulating the faith" and con-

---

[6] *Ibid.,* id.

[7] *Ibid.,* pp. 286-90.

[8] *Ibid.,* p. 208.

demned the use of "vague and ambiguous expressions." [9]
He asserted that from this point of view the statements of the
assembly were "worthless." [10] He nevertheless recognized
that some progress had been made since the preceding assembly. It had at least been possible to speak of the venera-
tion of the Virgin and the saints.[11] As a matter of fact notes
describing its divergence from the faith of the Orthodox
Church were added to the statements of the assembly.

The Synod of Moscow, which we have already mentioned,
took place shortly before the Amsterdam Assembly. Ecumenism was on the program of the synod.

Just as was the case with Anglican orders, the Moscow
Synod, following the lead of Patriarch Alexis, took a reverse
course in the matter of ecumenical relations. An ecumenism
which does not keep doctrine in the forefront, the Patriarch
stated, "does not seek the reunion of Churches through spiritual means." On the contrary, in seeking to become a force
capable of influencing international politics, it busies itself
primarily with social and political questions. But to do this
is to give in to the temptation to power that Christ rejected
in the desert. The Moscow Synod therefore decided not to
take any official part in the ecumenical movement such as it
was at the time.[12]

The Orthodox were nevertheless present at Amsterdam.
The Ecumenical Patriarch and the Greek Church, whose
representatives had not taken part in the doctrinal debates
at Moscow, sent delegates. The Russian Orthodox of the
United States, who are not under the jurisdiction of Patriarch
Alexis, did the same. Their participation in the debates at
Amsterdam was the same as at Lausanne and Edinburgh.
The delegates took an active part in the discussions. But they

---

[9] Leonard Hodgson (ed.), *The Second World Conference on
Faith and Order*, 1938, p. 156. The text of this protest is on pp.
154-8; *Istina*, 1955, pp. 180-3.
[10] *Ibid.*, p. 157.
[11] *Ibid.*, p. 156.
[12] See *Istina*, 1955, pp. 185-7.

always refused to make commitments in the name of their Churches. The Metropolitan of Thyatire, who once more presided over the Orthodox delegations, expressed this position in a special statement that he made to the Assembly: "We have to base ourselves especially on the way that the various Churches express themselves on occasion concerning the World Council of Churches and its aspirations." [13] In other words, the Orthodox are only taking a provisional stand in the World Council. A definitive position depends on a decision taken by the entire Orthodox Church to approve or condemn the Council. As long as such a decision has not been made one way or the other, there is nothing against provisional participation. But up to now Orthodoxy as such is not responsible for the decision made by some bishops, be it the Ecumenical Patriarch himself, in favor of participation. At the present time there is no sign of a world-wide decision in this matter.

Before the Lund Conference the Patriarch of Constantinople asked for the opinion of the Autocephalous Churches on three points: Should they take part in ecumenical conferences? Should the delegates discuss, or only explain, the Orthodox faith? Is it expedient to establish a new confession of faith in order to facilitate this participation? The theologians of the Church of Greece did not go to Lund. There were only delegates of the Ecumenical Patriarch and some Russian delegates from North America. The Patriarch had given strict instructions not to participate in any dogmatic debate. This was brought to the attention of the Assembly by Bishop Athenagoras, who succeeded Bishop Germanos as Metropolitan of Thyatire. The reason he gave for this restriction was that "the Hierarchy of the entire Greek Orthodox Church reserves for itself alone the right to decide what is wrong in religious matters and to pronounce what is compatible or incompatible with her faith." The Metropolitan

---

[13] Visser't Hooft (ed.), *The First Assembly of the World Council of Churches. Official Report*, 1949, p. 220; see *Istina*, 1955, pp. 187-8.

added that the Orthodox Church is "the whole and only Church, the Body of Christ, the only mandatory agent of the Apostles . . . the One, Holy, Catholic and Apostolic Church." [14]

The Orthodox delegates participated more freely in the debates at Evanston in 1954. The Greeks were with them this time. Some of them, such as Metropolitan Michael of the Greek Church of the United States and professor George Florovsky, spoke at the plenary sessions. The entire Orthodox delegation remained as inflexible as ever on the question of doctrine, however. Archbishop Michael read two statements indicating why the Orthodox would have no part in the doctrinal decisions of the Assembly. On August 25th he criticized the relevance of the report of the Congress on "Christ, the hope of the world." Among other things, he said: "If we seek at the present time in our troubled and distorted world, a true basis for human hope, we must profess emphatically that it is only in the Church of God, Holy, Catholic, and Apostolic, that this basis can be found, since the Church is the 'pillar and ground of Truth.' " [15] On August 29th he read a second declaration, criticizing the report drawn up by the Commission on Faith and Order on Church unity. This ended with a declaration of faith. "The Holy Orthodox Church alone has kept whole and entire the faith that was given to the saints once and for all." [16]

The Oberlin Conference in 1958 was no exception. Five American Orthodox groups were present. In the name of the Russian delegates Archbishop John of San Francisco wrote a letter of protest against the political implications of some of the debates. "I ask that you inform the members of the conference . . . that personally and as representative of the

---

[14] Oliver Tomkins (ed.), *The Third World Conference on Faith and Order*, 1953, pp. 123-6; see *Istina*, 1955, pp. 191-3.

[15] *The Evanston Report*, 1954, pp. 329-31.

[16] Text, *St. Vladimir Seminary Bulletin*, New York, Winter 1959, pp. 32-3.

Church that has delegated me, I can be responsible only for the statements and decisions of the conference that have nothing to do with questionable and mundane politics, and that are of undeniable importance to all Christians because they extol the Spirit of Christ, the spirit of sanctity, of humanity and of justice in this country and in the entire world." [17] This coincided with the fears expressed at the Synod of Moscow. There was danger that ecumenism should give in to the temptation to power and become a tool of American political action. On the doctrinal level, the Orthodox delegates again expressed their opposition to the Protestant concepts which prevailed in the documents of the Assembly. They abstained from voting on the message to the Churches. This message considered unity to be in the future and yet to be established. In the name of the Orthodox, Father Florovsky informed the Assembly that he and his colleagues could have no part in such a message.

The Orthodox who participate in the World Council of Churches thus take advantage of every occasion where they may state the traditional doctrine of Eastern Christianity before the Anglican and Protestant delegates. Those who do not attend the Council, particularly the Patriarchate of Moscow, follow the ecumenical movement with interest and possibly with anxiety. They are above all anxious to remain faithful to Orthodox unanimity. That is why they follow a policy of withdrawal in respect to ecumenism. Partly because of the pressure of circumstances and partly because of the admirable doctrinal conservatism of the Church in the Soviet Union, the position of the Orthodox within the World Council has become more delicate within the past few years than ever before. The movement that is bringing the Council to join with the Missionary Council causes disturbances among the Orthodox. If the World Council assumed the task of propagating Protestant interpretations of the faith, the Orthodox

---

[17] *Ibid.*

Churches could not associate themselves with such proselyting. Father Florovsky warned against this danger when the Central Committee of the World Council met at New Haven from July 30-August 7, 1957. As he pointed out, such a direction would change the nature of the Council and would force the Orthodox to revise the principle of their participation. The missionary concerns in the World Council being what they are, it is not likely that these warnings will in any respect change plans for union with the International Missionary Council. In spite of this, it is highly improbable that the Orthodox will quit the World Council. Yet their participation may take on a still more protesting character.

There is some promise of closer future cooperation between Russian Orthodoxy and ecumenism. The Patriarchate of Moscow itself is at present noticeably removed from the unshakeable position it held in 1948. From August 7-9, 1958, some representatives of Patriarch Alexis met with officers of the World Council at Utrecht. The latter were the Secretary General, Dr. Franklin Fry, an American Lutheran, and a Greek Orthodox bishop, James, the Metropolitan of Malta. The Russian delegation was made up of Nicolas, Metropolitan of Krutitsy, Michael, Bishop of Smolensk, and a layman, Alex Boejewsky, professor of theology at the Academy of Moscow. The purpose of the meeting was to establish contacts and to bring back to the Patriarch information on the possibility and conditions of a collaboration. On the part of ecumenism there is hope of thereby stabilizing Orthodox participation in the activities of the Council. There is also hope that friendly relations with the Patriarch of Moscow will perhaps make it possible later on to establish relations with Protestant groups in the Soviet Union, particularly Lutherans and Baptists.

Pending the development of such relations, the Church of the Soviet Union has been invited to send observers to future ecumenical assemblies, the meetings of the Central Committee of the Council included. In June and July of 1959

another Russian delegation paid a visit to the central office
of the World Council. Archpriest Vitaly Borovoy of the
Leningrad Theological Academy and Victor Alexeev of the
office of the Patriarchate of Moscow spent three weeks in
Geneva.

The intransigeance of the Synod of Moscow in 1948 has
been partly corrected in another respect. At that time the
Patriarch would not heed the Anglicans' desire to have their
ordinations recognized as valid. The doctrinal position has
not changed; yet friendly relations have been established
between Moscow and Canterbury since that time. In July,
1955, a Russian religious delegation made up of four Orthodox, two Lutherans, and two Baptists visited England. Pitirim,
Metropolitan of Minsk then invited the Anglican hierarchy
to send a delegation to Russia. A theological meeting to be
held in Moscow was organized. This took place July 16-23,
1956. Part of the time the Anglicans spent there was taken
up with a tour that acquainted them with the secular and
religious life of the USSR. The rest of their stay was occupied
with theological conferences. Among the subjects discussed
were the nature of the Church, Scripture and Tradition,
dogma, the *Filioque,* the number and nature of the sacraments, and liturgical rites.[18]

As it turned out, the theological discussions consisted in
comparisons and explanations. The Russian theologians did
not swerve from the traditional positions of Orthodoxy on
one single point. The question of Anglican orders was not
on the program and was not discussed. Russian Orthodoxy
had not altered its position since 1948. It had simply relaxed
its discipline in respect to contacts with the non-Orthodox
world. It is possible that political pressures had contributed
to bringing about this move.

Since then meetings of this sort have been on the increase.
A Russian Orthodox delegation from the USSR was

---

[18] See H. M. Waddams, (ed.), *The Anglo-Russian Theological
Conference, Moscow, July 1956,* 1958.

They thereby put the Catholic problem before the Protestant world and gave it a central place in world ecumenism. In the last analysis, the true ecumenical dialogue is not the dialogue of the Anglican and Protestant Churches among themselves. It is the dialogue that rises from the depths of Christian dissensions and establishes itself between the Reformed Church on the one hand and Catholicism and Orthodoxy on the other. The more the ecumenical movement becomes aware of this, the greater the depths it will gain. It must give increasing importance to the Catholic and Orthodox objection to Protestant negations. In this respect Orthodoxy and Catholicism share a common cause.

This offers promise of some degree of closer relationships between Orthodoxy and Catholicism. Theological agreements between the two have always been good, even if official relations have been poor and the two Churches have tended to ignore each other. Whatever may have happened in the distant past, Catholicism must recognize Orthodoxy for the courage and constancy of its doctrinal witness. The fidelity of the Orthodox to the ancient tradition is a precious guarantee of ecumenical relations in the future.

present at the Assembly of the Central Committee of th World Council held at Rhodes in August, 1959. Archpries Vitaly Borovoy and M. Victor Alexeev were present as offi cial observers, and Metropolitan Nicolas addressed a lette to the Central Committee that was filled with understandin and sympathy. In his message he took care to put the Worl Council on its guard against one of its ever-present tempta tions. "I think it necessary," he said, "to express the hope that the social concern of the World Council of Churches will not overshadow the main task of the ecumenical move ment, which aims at the unity of the faith, which is divided by differing interpretations." [19]

A short time thereafter, in November and December, 1959, five delegates of the World Council, including Dr. Visser't Hooft, spent some weeks in the Soviet Union as guests of the Orthodox Church. In his farewell address Patriarch Alexis expressed his desire to see the bonds draw closer between the Russian Church and other Christians: "We shall strengthen our spiritual friendship while endeavouring to reveal to you the treasures of our ancient faith transmitted to us by the Apostles and Fathers of the Church. . . . Our strength lies in the sacraments of the Church through the mystery of which comes the unseen but real presence of the Lord Himself among us. . . . That strength does not come from ourselves. It proceeds from the quickening grace of the Holy Spirit, and is due to the guidance of Divine Provi dence leading Christ's Church by ways inscrutable, known to God alone." [20]

From the Catholic viewpoint, the theological contribution that the Orthodox have made to the ecumenical dialogue is extremely valuable. Whatever they may be in the World Council or apart from it, the Orthodox bishops and theo logians are faithful to the sacramental and ecclesiological tradition that they have inherited from the Greek Fathers.

[19] *Ecumenical Press Service,* September 4, 1959, p. 9.
[20] *Ecumenical Press Service,* December 22, 1959, p. 6.

CHAPTER XVIII

THE FINAL QUESTION

> *"Never agree to the scandal of Christian divisions, that*
> *glibly proclaim love for their neighbor but remain*
> *divided. Have love for the unity of Christ's Body."*
> —The Rule of Taizé

The Orthodox and Roman Catholic Churches share the
privilege of defending Catholic principles in the ecumenical
dialogue. No other Church is basically committed to fidelity
to Tradition. No other Church is exempt from what the
Catholics and Orthodox, in the light of the great councils,
judge to be heresies. Ecumenical dialogues between the
various Churches therefore divide up into two camps. On
the one hand we have the Catholic tradition of Orthodoxy
and Roman Catholicism, and on the other hand the various
Anglican and Protestant traditions issuing from the sixteenth
century Reformation.

The situation is nevertheless more complicated than it
would at first seem. The dialogue betwen Churches is far
from being perfect. Representatives of the Churches in the
World Council do not commit their respective denominations
and fellow Church members whenever they express an opin-

211

ion. They are official delegates but their decisions, if they make any, have not the force of law and remain subject to the judgment of the Churches themselves. Neither the Orthodox community nor the Catholic Church engages in any formal debates with Protestantism.

In addition to this there are various doctrinal currents within many of the Churches. Anglicanism is the best known case. Its "High Church" theologians have concepts that are widely different from those of the "evangelical" or "Low Church" persuasion. Varying interpretations of Christian and Protestant matters are to be found in the Protestant Churches themselves. In Lutheranism, particularly German and Swedish Lutheranism, "High Church" movements have introduced a liturgical revival. They have attempted to maintain together the two poles of Luthern thought: fidelity to the Reformation, and concern for the earlier tradition. Even within Calvinism some schools of thought are closer to Catholic tradition than others. Karl Barth, while not close to Catholicism, has started a doctrinal revival that has affected Protestantism throughout Europe. The English Congregationalists have also experienced a "High Church" theology associated with the names of Charles Dodd and Daniel Jenkins. A theology that is faithful to Calvin, anxious about patristic tradition, and at the same time deeply concerned over Christian unity has become popularized among Swiss and French Protestants through the review *Verbum Caro*. Its life can be observed at the Protestant monastery of Taizé-les-Cluny.

A study of ecumenism should not be kept, therefore, within the defined limits of official Church activities however broad these may be. Theological experiments and methods that seek to make the Church receptive to a deeper catholicity also have their place, no matter how insignificant they may be.

Anglicanism has always been distinguished from Protestantism. Anglican theologians of the seventeenth century are the distant ancestors of Anglo-Catholicism, the most

advanced trend in modern Anglicanism.[1] The central point
in their doctrine is the concept that the true Church must
be at once Catholic and Protestant. It is to be Protestant by
its constant anxiety to reform itself and Catholic in its
sources of faith and its forms of worship. The Oxford Movement, which was the Anglican renewal of the nineteenth
century, insisted on the continuity of the Catholic tradition
in the Anglican Communion. Its basic elements are carried
on in modern Anglo-Catholicism. Scholars like Gregory Dix
(1901-52) or T. G. Jalland have tried to justify it by means
of historical studies, while E. L. Mascall finds inspiration in
the Thomistic tradition, and G. Hebert and Sir Edwyn
Hoskyns (1884-1937) are devoted to scriptural exegesis.
Austin Farrar devotes himself to outstanding exegetical syn-
theses, poetry, metaphysics, and theology. In the case of
J. V. L. Casserley, Anglo-Catholicism combines theology and
sociology, and L. S. Thornton studies the scriptural and
patristic sources of doctrinal orthodoxy.

Present-day Anglo-Catholic theology makes up an ensemble
of the highest calibre. It can be aptly described by saying that
it has restored the concept of tradition as a norm of faith.
In this sense it is certainly "Catholic." It is not based solely
on Scripture, but mainly on the witness of the past centuries,
particularly the patristic age, and that of the Catholic liturgies,
both Latin and Byzantine. This tradition of the undivided
Church is for Anglo-Catholicism today the true interpretation
of the Church and therefore the norm for all doctrines, as it
was in former times.

It is self-evident that this central principle must engender
a special conception of ecumenism. No matter whether it be

---

[1] On Anglicanism and Anglo-Catholicism see Yves Congar,
Brêve Histoire des Courants de Pensée dans L'Anglicanisme, in
Istina, 1957, pp. 133-64; André Tolédano, *Histoire de l'Angleterre
Chrétienne*, 1955; and Stanislas Cwiertniack, *La Vierge Marie dans
la Tradition Anglicane*, 1958. For the Oxford Movement, see P.
Thureau-Dangin, *La Renaissance Catholique en Angleterre au XIXe
siècle*, 3 vol., 1899-1906.

more inclined to the side of Rome or to that of Byzantium, Anglo-Catholicism sees ecumenism as a problem of reintegration. Tradition as a norm must be restored to Protestantism. The entire Christian world must return to the tradition of the undivided Church. Certainly, Christian unity is a goal that lies ahead of us, but only because it is first of all behind us. We can march ahead only by referring to the landmarks of the past. As Mascall insists, one should *reculer pour mieux sauter:* draw back for a better leap. In his book, *The Recovery of Unity* (1958), Mascall asserts that modern Christianity needs to go back to its origins. Byzantium and Rome have also been unfaithful to the ancient tradition, and not just the Reformation. They have not all been unfaithful in the same way. Yet each member of severed Christianity has something with which to reprimand the others. But unless they all bring themselves to rediscover the Catholic unity of the patristic age a dialogue between the Churches today will remain a dialogue between deaf-mutes. Mascall thinks that Roman Catholicism should develop an ecclesiology that is primarily sacramental rather than juridical.[2] Orthodoxy has need of self-criticism.[3] Protestantism must rediscover the meaning of organic Christianity, completely forgotten by the individualism of the Reformation. Only a return to the Catholicism of the Fathers of the Church will make Christian reunion possible. It calls for the development of an ecumenism that starts at the roots, not with the branches.

This analysis of the unifying centre of ecumenism naturally leads to defining the return to sources necessary to Christian reunion. Thornton has done a masterly job of this.[4] For him, the structure of orthodoxy as based on the writings of the Fathers comprises three elements. There are Scripture and Tradition and to these must be added the Cosmic Order.

---

[2] *The Recovery of Unity*, p. 232.
[3] *Ibid.*, pp. 52-64.
[4] See *The Forms of the Servant* (3 vols.), particularly the first volume, *Revelation and the Modern World,* 1950.

All three reveal God. In the first centuries of the Church these three were inseparable. The Church is the milieu in which Scripture and the Cosmos together present the Word of God to man. But today, Thornton feels, the rupture of Christian unity has separated these three inseparable elements of the structural unity of orthodoxy. Catholicism prefers the perspective of "Tradition." Doctrinal Protestantism gives first place to the biblical aspects of orthodoxy. The Cosmic Order, which was secularized towards the end of the Middle Ages, predominates in liberal Protestantism. The latter is clearly unorthodox. Doctrinal Protestantism and Catholicism on the other hand, whether Eastern or Western, are two forms of orthodoxy, neither of which has preserved the full proportions of Revelation in its entirety. The path to unity involves a rediscovery of complete orthodoxy, on the part of both Catholicism and Protestantism. A parallel effort must be made to find out what kind of tradition is truly complementary to the Scripture-Cosmos unity. The present revival of biblical studies makes a reading of the Bible possible that reinstates the Word of God in the human and cosmic setting that serves as its medium. Ecumenism has to complete this renewal by defining what ecclesiastical and sacramental milieu must serve as the medium of Scripture and the spiritual purpose of the world in our day.

Therefore Anglo-Catholic theologians emphasize doctrinal ecumenism more than practical ecumenism. They investigate what kinds of theological study are capable of transforming the Protestant-Catholic conflict into a dialogue that will serve as a means of leading from division to unity.

Unfortunately Anglo-Catholicism has not enjoyed any degree of influence in ecumenical circles up to the present time. Roman Catholics are hardly aware of its existence. Yet it is too close to them for Protestants to have much confidence in it, so Anglo-Catholicism rarely comes to the fore in the official statements of the World Council of Churches. Its hesitation, in fact its opposition to projects for union such as that in South India, where doctrine is put aside, impede its participation in the ecumenical movement. Within Anglicanism itself Anglo-Catholicism competes with the Protestantism of the "Evangelical" trend that is generally favored by the Anglican hierarchy. It does not have enough influence with the administration of the Anglican Churches to check the "latitudinarianism" that the Anglican bishops evidenced in the South India question. In 1955, over Anglo-Catholic protests, the Convocations of Canterbury and York voted in favor of partial intercommunion with the Church of South India. An American Anglican, William H. Dunphy, aptly expressed the Anglo-Catholic position on the question:

"The answer to a one-sided distortion of Christianity is not an equally one-sided distortion in another direction, but the presentation of Christian truth in its fulness, in its Catholicity. The South India scheme fails because it seeks a reunion of Christendom on a minimal instead of a maximal basis, the basis of Catholicity. But the true Church of Christ is the Body and the fulness of Him who is full of grace and truth." [5]

Anglo-Catholicism is a renewing force within Anglicanism despite its limited influence on the practical attitude shown by Anglican prelates towards dubious projects of union. It nourishes its liturgical movement and keeps alive its interest in patristic theology. It thereby assures the beginning of a return to sources without which there can be no living ecumenism. It therefore represents a very valuable potential for ecumenism. This is the direction in which we must seek the path of an ecumenism that will do full justice to the Catholic tradition.

No other catholicizing movement has attained the breadth

---

[5] William H. Dunphy, *The Episcopal Church and the Church of South India*, reprinted from *The Star in the East*, November, 1956, by *The American Church Union*, New York. pp. 5-6.

of Anglo-Catholicism. No other is as venerable, inasmuch as Anglo-Catholicism traces its origins back to the Reformation of Henry VIII and from thence back to pre-Reformation Catholicism. However, there are groups in other parts of the Christian world that are trying to restore doctrines and practices that were abandoned since the Reformation. They do not go so far back in history as Anglo-Catholicism. They do not enjoy a historic continuity with ancient Catholicism. They nevertheless strive to rediscover some Catholic values. This rediscovery and search for Catholicity inevitably brings up the question of Catholicism. This explains the growth of more or less important centres, within Lutheran or Calvinist Protestantism, where the ecumenical question is seen principally in terms of Rome. Instead of looking primarily towards the World Council of Churches here, there is hope of a truly ecumenical reunion in a resumption of relations with the Catholic Church.

The most noteworthy of these movements was born in German Lutheranism shortly after the end of the last war. Its progression can be traced in the *Hoch Kirche* movement that developed in Germany after the First World War and which was principally connected with the name of Professor Friedrich Heiler. The protest made by the Confessing Church during the Hitlerian era against national socialist paganism soon purified these aspirations which were still tainted with religious romanticism. This renewal of the Lutheran Church would be purely religious and completely concerned with the domain of faith. After the ordeals of the Second World War the future founders of "The Gathering" *(Die Sammlung)* perceived that Lutheranism needed a complete renovation. They began to shape their views from about 1945, when all the German Churches were anxiously wondering about the future.

Gradually this group of theologians launched a movement of self-criticism that would help German Lutheranism examine itself in the light of Catholicism. This movement was inaugurated in January, 1954, by an open letter. This was followed by six others which appeared at irregular intervals up until May, 1957. "The Gathering" expanded. Only a small circle at first, it has developed into a society described as follows: " *'Die Sammlung'* is an association of Lutherans, men and women, clergy and laity, who have heard the divine appeal for the reunion of severed Christianity and who work and pray in the hope that for their perfection and for the future good of the Church of God, the Reformation Churches may find their indispensable place in the one, holy, catholic and apostolic Church." "The Gathering" therefore had an ecumenical purpose. It had in mind a Lutheran-Catholic rapprochement with a view to the future reintegration of the Reformation into the one Church. Before such a reintegration could take place, two conditions must be fulfilled. Catholics on the one hand must give due recognition to the Catholic truths that the Lutheran Reformation conserves or even emphasizes. Lutherans on the other hand must realize that in itself the Reformation is not justified. It has no significance apart from its relation with the Catholic Church. Lutheranism in its deepest *raison d'être* has but one aim: to emphasize Catholic truths that were left obscure towards the end of the Middle Ages. It consequently would not be right in maintaining a separate existence if the Church of Rome gave these Catholic truths their rightful place. "The Gathering" raises the following question: Is the Church of Rome sufficiently reformed to make the Lutheran protest unnecessary? This gives rise to a connected question: Has Lutheranism remained faithful to its original intention of purifying the faith?

In practice, "The Gathering" organizes study days about twice a year. It keeps its members and friends in contact with one another by means of a bulletin. The series of seven open letters issued between January, 1954, and May, 1957, is still the most important enterprise it has undertaken up to date.

The first of these letters, signed by Hans Asmussen, Max

Lackmann and Wolfgang Lehmann, points the question of Christian unity in terms of a unity between Lutherans and Catholics. "We know that the truth still separates us. But we also know that the truth separates the Churches and Lutheran theologians from one another as well. And from this point of view our relation with the Roman Catholic Church is no exception." There is unity in Lutheranism in spite of diversity in respect to the truth. Why should not an analogous unity be established with Catholicism? "We ask our Catholic brethren to tell us why the confession of faith that separates us from them should keep us from participating in the light of Christ as they do." [6]

The second letter was at Easter, 1954, and explained the catholic meaning of the central teachings of Lutheranism. *"Christ alone* means Christ and the Church; *by grace alone* means God and the saints." [7] As for *Scripture alone,* this by no means hinders "the interpretation of Scripture from having a historical norm." [8] The letters of February 17th and August 18, 1956, recalled the urgency of the question raised by "The Gathering" in the light of current events. The letter of Advent, 1956, spoke of the growth of "The Gathering" and mentioned happily that the number of "those who regret our separation from the Mother Church of the West" is increasing.[9] The sixth letter, of Lent, 1957, repeated a message received from the Soviet Zone of Germany. The last letter, of May 16, 1957, returned to the doctrinal exposé of the first two. It set down the following principle: "That alone is Christian which is universally Christian; that which is Catholic is Christian, and that which is separated is not Christian. The mission of our age is to look for that which is truly Catholic." [10] The letter then defined the meaning of

---

[6] Hans Asmussen, *The Unfinished Reformation,* 1960, Fides Publishers.

[7] *Ibid.*

[8] *Ibid.*

[9] *Ibid.*

[10] *Ibid.*

the following points as understood by "The Gathering": The Word of God, the Incarnation, grace and freedom, the mystery of the Church, the Head and the members, the sacrifice of Christ and that of the Church, the apostolic succession, the priesthood, the government of the Church, Scripture and Tradition, the magisterium, and the communion of saints.

The position taken by *Die Sammlung* in respect to modern Catholicism is friendly but critical. "The Gathering" would also like Roman Catholicism to take up some of the questions currently raised in Lutheranism. In 1956 Hans Asmussen proposed "five questions to the Catholic Church" that he thought would facilitate relations with Lutheranism.[11] These questions were mainly concerned with the Catholic attitude towards the Lutheran Church. "Does the Catholic Church really believe that a properly administered Lutheran baptism can never be repeated? What does the Christianity that is common to both Confessions consist in? What do you think of what is Christian among us? What do you think of our Eucharist?" These questions led to a more fundamental one, namely "Does that which is Catholic take precedence over what is Christian?"

"The Gathering" hoped to get Catholics and Lutherans together by means of a parallel return to the fountains of living water of the Catholic tradition. It has met with inevitable opposition within Protestantism. In 1956 Richard Baumann, one of its chief leaders, was deprived of his post as pastor in the Lutheran Church of Würtemberg.[12] But "The Gather-

---

[11] The text is in *Una Sancta*, Sept. 1956, pp. 127-30. At the conclusion of his book *Rom, Wittemberg, Moscau*, Asmussen puts five further questions to the Catholic Church. These have to do with Catholic doctrine on (1) The Word and the sacraments; (2) theology and philosophy; (3) redemptive causality; (4) Christ and law; (5) Mariology (*op. cit.*, pp. 148-56). Heinrich Fries has published an answer to these questions: *Antwort an Asmussen*, 1958.

[12] Baumann's doctrine, condemned by the Würtemberg Church Council (*Oberkirchenrat*), is simply that Christ founded His Church on Peter, the Rock. See Richard Baumann, *Fels der Welt*, 1956.

ing" has survived the crisis of those years of conflict. The publications of its members have put it in the forefront of Lutheran theology as far as ecumenism is concerned.[13] This has given it status. It has put the Catholic question before German Lutheranism. Its influence has even spread beyond the boundaries of Germany. During its congress at Minneapolis in 1957, the Lutheran World Federation decided to open an institute for the study of modern Catholicism. It felt that Lutheranism has no right to a separate existence unless its protest is justified by the present state of Catholicism.

An ecumenism having Catholic tendencies has even appeared in Calvinism. A movement related to "The Gathering" has existed in Holland since 1946. After a number of meetings the "Hilversum Group" as it called itself, published a statement of principles in 1950 that caused a commotion in Dutch Calvinism. In 1952 it erected itself into a legal association.

The "Hilversum Group" is characterized by both a liturgical and an ecclesiological aspect. As for the liturgy, it wishes to restore a prayer like the Roman breviary, and its annual reunions are prayer meetings as well as theological meetings. In regard to ecclesiology, it aims to recover for its Church an episcopal hierarchy duly constituted to pass on the apostolic succession. As the 1950 declaration stated, "we believe that a true religious and ecclesiological future for our people is hopeless unless we consciously strive to re-establish contact with the historic order of doctrine and Christian life, of the faith and government of the Church from which we are definitely convinced that we are at present separated." Thus the "Hilversum Group" hopes that the Reformed Church will gradually orientate itself towards an episcopal form of government, a liturgical restoration and a doctrinal reformation

---

Have the members of the *Oberkirchenrat* never read the book by Lutheran Oscar Cullmann called *Pierre, apôtre, disciple, martyr?* 1952.

[13] Hans Asmussen is particularly influential.

leading to a rediscovery of catholic truths. It differs from *Die Sammlung* inasmuch as it does not seek catholicity primarily in Roman Catholic terms. It looks up rather to the Anglican Communion.[14]

French Calvinism has no movement comparable to "The Gathering," and no one dreams of asking for apostolic succession from the Church of England. The movement for a return to doctrinal sources that centers around the review *Verbum Caro* is nevertheless worth mention. It is concerned with a new reform of the Reformation, a task true to the spirit of real Calvinism. This time neither Roman Catholicism nor Anglicanism are taken as models, but the Gospel, read in the light of Church history as seen in the Catholic as well as the Reformed tradition. The profoundly Christian meaning of some elements that the Reformation rid itself of in the sixteenth century have thus reappeared. This liturgical and doctrinal awakening flourishes in the Monastery of Taizé. "Let us be a sign of brotherly love and of joy among men," the Rule of Taizé enjoins. The ecumenical spirit of Taizé has been a sign of brotherly love and of joy among Catholic and Protestant Christians as well as among Protestants of various Churches. Its theological influence, particularly through the writings of Max Thurian, fosters a renewal of liturgical life.

Calvinism and Lutheranism are therefore contributing to the development of an ecumenism that really states the Catholic question. This question was raised in Anglicanism long ago, and Anglo-Catholicism has a firm footing and a large audience today. *Die Sammlung* appears to be more clearly

---

[14] The leading figures in the "Hilversum Group" are J. Loos, pastor at Hilversum, and J. N. Bakhuisen van den Brink, professor at the University of Leyden. The declaration of principles together with some commentaries appeared originally under the title of "Reformation and Catholicity." The commentaries were written by ten ministers of the Reformed Church (*Hervormde*) of Holland. There is an English translation: *Reformation and Catholicity*, New York, 1954. Quotation, p. 7.

oriented in this direction than the "Hilversum Group." It tackles directly the doctrinal aspect of an ecumenism where Catholicism plays a role. It might possibly be reproached with forgetting that a Calvinist Christianity also exists. But it would no doubt answer that the way to reform begins by reforming oneself. Its self-appointed task is to reform Lutheranism and to leave the reformation of Calvinism to others. The "Hilversum Group" attempts such a reform of Dutch Calvinism. It raises the problem first on the liturgical and institutional level, and this gives it a less secure footing, for this clashes with habits of thought and sensibilities that are oftentimes more deeply rooted than doctrinal prejudices. The Monastery of Taizé has more limited aims. It only wants to bear witness to Christianity by its life, example, and words, without founding a movement. Its influence depends on its spontaneous radiance. And the monastic life cannot help but lead back towards its patristic and medieval sources as well as towards its sources in the New Testament.

We have repeatedly remarked that true ecumenism must take on the form of a dialogue between the Protestant and the Catholic tradition. Such a dialogue is presently underway in the movements described in this chapter with far greater force than in the official ecumenism of the World Council of Churches. These and other circles that may rise in the future are the heralds of hope for a rapprochement between Catholicism and Protestantism which should be an anticipation of the final ecumenism.

CHAPTER XIX

TOWARDS A COUNCIL

*"Fidelity to the tradition of the past is a guarantee of
future happiness."*

—John XXIII

After the pontificate of Leo XIII allusions to the ecumenical
problem appeared less frequently in the documents of his
immediate successor, Pius X. Benedict XV took up the
question again. Pius XI made a great step forward in ecumenical method when he outlined, at least as regards Orthodoxy, the general plan of a calmly irenic ecumenism. The
generous interest that Pius XII took in all the big problems
of the world also directed his thoughts towards ecumenism.
But it was inevitable that the Pope's strong personality would
lead him to take up these problems in his own way. There
are, to be sure, many expressions to be found in the writings
and discourses of Pius XII that follow closely what his predecessors since Leo XIII had said on this subject. Nevertheless
Pius XII does not put the emphasis where Pius XI, Benedict
XV or Leo XIII did. On the one hand, the situation created
by the formation of the World Council of Churches was

completely new. On the other hand, the international crisis that the world was passing through gave Christian differences a new perspective. Finally, there was the Holy Father's personality. Formed in diplomacy, an expert in Canon Law, and deeply interested in social and political questions, he gave very studied attention to certain factors of disunion, particularly the question of relations between Church and State. Though this may not be the main problem of ecumenism, it is relevant.

Ecumenism was therefore taken up indirectly during the pontificate of Pius XII therefore. The movement had become so widespread that it was impossible to ignore officially the existence of the World Council of Churches, whose activities were known throughout the world.

The Pope's customary practice of occasionally inviting all Christians to rediscover Christian unity in the Roman Catholic Communion continued. On June 29, 1943, such an appeal was formulated in the encyclical *Mystici corporis.* "We ask each and every one of them to correspond to the interior movements of grace . . . may they enter into Catholic unity, and, joined with Us in the one, organic Body of Jesus Christ, may they all be gathered together under the one Head in a glorious communion of love." Similar appeals were directed towards the Orthodox Churches on a number of occasions. April 9, 1944, was the fifteenth centenary of the death of St. Cyril of Alexandria *(Orientalis Ecclesiae decus).* As a protest over the enforced transference of the Ruthenians to the jurisdiction of the Patriarch of Moscow and by way of renewing his invitation to unity *(Orientales omnes),* the Pope celebrated on December 23, 1945, the 350th anniversary of the Brest-Litovsk union, which brought the Ruthenian Church into union with Rome. The encyclical *Sempiternus Rex,* written for the fifteenth centenary of the Council of Chalcedon (September 8, 1951), took up the theme of union: "We foresee what a rich source of blessings for the common welfare of Christianity this return to the unity of the Church would be." On July 7, 1952, Pius XII addressed an encyclical to the people of Russia, *Sacro vergente anno*. In it he remarked that "up until 1448 no official document declared your Church to be separated from the Apostolic See." [1] In saying this the Pope placed the date of the separation from Rome as late as possible. Unity was one of the subjects discussed in *Orientales Ecclesias* (December 15, 1952), an encyclical on the religious persecution in Eastern Europe.

These invitations are classics of pontifical writings. They indicate the purpose of the movement towards unity as understood by Catholic tradition. But the best method to arrive at this end is yet to be determined, and this is the task of Catholic ecumenism.

A second aspect of the mind of Pius XII in the matter of Christian reunion is concerned with his many pleas for all disciples of Christ to work together despite the barriers that separate the Christian denominations. In his numerous allocutions, especially his admirable Christmas messages, the Sovereign Pontiff insisted on the common interests of all Christians in the defense of the spiritual heritage of humanity. He addressed himself to "all those who, without belonging to the visible body of the Catholic Church, are close to us by faith in God and Jesus Christ" (Christmas, 1941).

These invitations had in mind primarily the work of social justice and international peace which, according to the mind of Pius XII, involved all Christians caught up in the net of the Second World War and its consequences. But in modern society several religious institutions coexist within the same State. The question of their cooperation toward social or civic goals is a matter of everyday life. This led the Pope to take up the problem of religious pluralism. In certain countries, especially in the United States, it is a thorny problem that occasions a great deal of writing and periodically upsets Catholic-Protestant relations. To what extent can Cath-

---

[1] *Documentation Catholique*, August 24, 1952, n. 1128, col. 1028.

olics agree with the idea of a neutral or secular State which considers all religions equal? The ecumenical get-together requires a positive answer to this question. Protestants and Catholics cannot collaborate without hesitation and some mutual fear. All claim to accept the pluralism of modern society without wanting to change its structures, yet the fear remains that a confessional state be imposed on others even through democratic means.

Pius XII is to be credited with taking an open-minded position in favour of mutual tolerance within the State. The allocution he gave on December 6, 1953, to the Fifth National Convention of the Union of Italian Catholic Jurists is remarkable in this respect. In it Pius XII took up "one of the questions which arise in a community of peoples, that is, the practical co-existence of Catholic with non-Catholic." [2] The problem concerned directly the relations between States where a majority of the citizens are "Christian, non-Christian, indifferent to religion or consciously without it, or even professedly atheist." [3] "Could it be," Pius XII asked, "that in certain circumstances [God] would not give men any mandate, would not impose any duty, and would not even communicate the right to impede or to repress what is erroneous and false? A look at things as they are gives an affirmative answer. . . . Hence the affirmation: 'Religious and moral error must always be impeded when it is possible because toleration of them is in itself immoral,' is not valid absolutely and unconditionally. The duty of repressing moral and religious error cannot therefore be an ultimate norm of action. It must be subordinate to higher and more general norms, which in some circumstances permit, and even perhaps seem to indicate as the better policy, toleration of error in order to promote a greater good." [4] To state it in another way, tolerance of religious beliefs that are thought to be erroneous

---

[2] *The Pope Speaks,* vol. 1, no. 1 (Spring, 1951), col. 4, p. 67.
[3] *Ibid.*
[4] *Ibid.,* col. 5, p. 68.

is, in some instances, an obligation. The Church herself practices this "for higher and more cogent motives," [5] that is to say, in order to safeguard the common good.

Pius XII thereby justified the existing pluralism of modern society. The common temporal good requires that opposed opinions and convictions coexist peacefully within a single society.

If then, the Church continues to condemn error, it nevertheless respects the right of the State to protect freedom of belief. Thus Pius XII takes up the thought of Leo XIII on relations between the two sovereign powers of Church and State. He referred to it explicitly in his allocution to the Tenth International Congress of Historical Sciences on September 7, 1955. On this occasion Pius XII dealt with Church-State relations. Catholics are often reproached by Protestants with having evolved tardily and unwillingly a doctrine of separation of Church and State. Pius XII did not share this way of thinking. "One might say that with the exception of a few centuries, throughout the whole of the first thousand years of Christian history, as during the last four centuries, the formula of Leo XIII more or less explicitly reflects the conscience of the Church. Moreover, even during the intermediary period there were representatives of the doctrine of the Church, and perhaps even the majority, who shared this same opinion." [6] In applying this formula the fact of pluralism must necessarily be taken into account. "The Church also knows however, that for some time now events have been developing in rather the other sense; that is to say, towards the multiplicity of religious confessions and concepts of life in the same national community, where Catholics constitute a more or less strong minority." [7] This pluralism is not justified in terms of the non-existent "rights of error." It is justified by the fact that the State, and even the Church, has a

---

[5] *Ibid.,* col. 6, p. 70.
[6] *Op. cit.,* vol. 2, no. 3 (Autumn, 1955), p. 210.
[7] *Ibid.,* p. 211.

responsibility towards the common good of all the people. Furthermore, it is implied in the subjective nature of the concrete moral obligation. "The Church believes that the convictions (of non-Catholics) constitute a motive, though not always the principal motive, of tolerance." [8]

Pius XII cleared up the atmosphere between Protestants and Catholics by offering a positive solution to a problem that formerly poisoned relations between separated Christians and which still does in some places. This is, as it were, pre-ecumenism, but it constitutes an indispensable preparation for fully ecumenical attitudes.

The pontificate of Pius XII marked progress in Catholic ecumenism in still one other respect. Under the Pope's leadership the *magisterium* officially recognized the ecumenical movement: It goes without saying that the preceding Popes had kept themselves informed on current events. Benedict XV and Pius XI had even been directly or indirectly in contact with some organizers of ecumenical assemblies. In his encyclical *Mortalium animos,* Pius XI mentioned it explicitly. But in view of the circumstances of his time and the existing condition of the ecumenical movement, he took a negative attitude towards it.

With Pius XII the official attitude of the Catholic hierarchy took a decidedly positive turn. It is true that no observers were sent to the Amsterdam (1948) and Evanston (1954) Asemblies. Yet, with all necessary authorization, several priests attended the Assemblies at Lund (1952) and Oberlin (1958) as well as the meeting of the Central Committee of the World Council at Nyborg (1958). But in the first instances, absence did not imply indifference. In July, 1948, on the occasion of the Amsterdam Assembly, the Dutch bishops published a pastoral letter. When the Evanston Assembly met, the Archbishop of Chicago also addressed his people, although his letter did not evidence as accurate a knowledge

---

[8] *Ibid.*

of the ecumenical movement as that of the Dutch bishops. It nonetheless showed that Catholics were concerned about Christian divisions. In any case, a long list of episcopal documents that treat of ecumenism with a great deal of understanding can be drawn up.[9]

Pius XII was not satisfied with a wait-and-see attitude. Through the Sacred Congregation of the Holy Office he published an instruction on the ecumenical movement which is the official charter, so far, of Catholic ecumenism. The instruction *Ecclesia Catholica* of September 20, 1949, contains three principal points. The first is an appreciation of the ecumenical movement, recognizing in it the mark of the Holy Spirit:

> "In many parts of the world, whether because of external events and a change of disposition, or rather because of the common prayers of the faithful, under the inspiration of the grace of the Holy Spirit, the desire that all those who believe in Christ our Lord return to unity has grown stronger day by day in the hearts of many who are separated from the Catholic Church." [10]

The bishops were then invited to work actively in the ecumenical movement:

> "They must not be content to observe this movement diligently and carefully, but must promote and direct it prudently, first of all by assisting those who seek the truth and the true Church, and second by protecting the faithful from

---

[9] Among others we may mention Bp. Michel Buchberger, Bishop of Regensburg, *Aufbruch zur Einheit und Einigkeit im Glauben*, 1948; Bp. Albert Stohr, Bishop of Mainz, pastoral letter of May 22, 1952; Bp. François Charrière, Bishop of Lausanne, pastoral letters of January 1958, July 1958, January 1959; a number of bishops have promoted participation in the January Unity Octave of Prayer, for ex., Cardinal Montini, Abp. of Milan, in January 1955; Bp. Jules Döpfner, Bishop of Wurzburg, in 1955 and 1956; Cardinal Saliege, Abp. of Tolouse, in January 1956, etc.

[10] *Documentation Catholique*, March 12, 1950, col. 330.

the dangers that easily result from the activity of this movement." [11]

The third point gives practical and theoretical rules regarding ecumenical meetings between Catholics and other Christians.

By the instruction *Ecclesia Catholica* the Holy See brought encouragement to Catholic ecumenists. Moreover, its publication corresponded with the development of a theology of ecumenism. The "Catholic Conference for Ecumenical Questions" was founded shortly afterwards, in 1952. This same instruction showed the Orthodox, the Anglicans, and the Protestants who work anxiously side by side in the World Council of Churches, that if the Catholic Church does not take an active part in their labors, she wants her bishops and theologians to share in the promotion of a true ecumenism.

The beginning of the pontificate of John XXIII is still too recent to allow for the perspective necessary to the historian. The first few months were enough, however, to give a new turn to Catholic ecumenism. This came with the announcement of an Ecumenical Council that would, among other things, be concerned with the problem of Christian reunions.

His Holiness Pope John XXIII has the advantage of approaching ecumenism with a personal experience of Orthodox Christianity. He spent ten years as apostolic delegate at Sofia, the capital of Bulgaria, and about the same length of time at Istanbul, the very seat of the Ecumenical Patriarch. Besides this, his sojourn in Paris as apostolic nuncio gave him an immediate acquaintance with the theology of ecumenism as it had developed in France. Thus for John XXIII, ecumenism is bound up with personal experiences more than was the case with his predecessors. It is interesting to note how, on December 24, 1934, while on his mission in Bul-

---

[11] *Ibid.*, col. 331.

garia, Bishop Roncalli described his attitude towards Orthodox Christians:

"The difference of religious beliefs regarding one of the
fundamental points in Christ's doctrine that we meet in
the Gospel, namely, the union of all the faithful of Christ's
Church with the successor of the Prince of the Apostles,
has brought me to exercise some reserve in my relations
and my personal behaviour with these separated brethren.
It was only natural. And I think I have been well understood, even by them. The fact that I have always tried to
show respect to each and every one by my inoffensive silence, both in public and in private, and the fact that I have
never bent down to pick up the stone that somebody threw
at me on the street, gives me the calm certitude that I
proved to all of them that I also love them in Christ with
the brotherly, profound, and sincere love that the Gospel
teaches us. The day must finally come when there will be
but one flock and one shepherd, because Jesus Christ so
wills it. Let us hasten the coming of this blessed day by
our prayers." [12]

In addition to this respectful and friendly irenicism and
his experience of living among the Orthodox, Cardinal Roncalli brings his knowledge of the Fathers of the Church, since
he used to be a professor of patrology. He also possesses a
rare historical knowledge of the Reformation and the Counter-Reformation. He is in fact well known in scholarly circles
as a historian of St. Charles Borromeo. The large volumes of
his edition of the acts of the apostolic visit of St. Charles
Borromeo to Bergamo make John XXIII a specialist in the
Council of Trent and the Counter-Reformation in Italy.

This should help us to understand John XXIII's decision
to convoke an ecumenical council. He has felt compelled to
say that this decision was born of "an inspiration which
struck Us in the humility of Our heart, like an unexpected

---

[12] *D.C.*, February 15, 1959, n. 1297, col. 200.

and irresistible command." [13] The councils held at the close of the Middle Ages and during the Renaissance were the instruments *par excellence* of the disciplinary reform of the Church. John XXIII gave a new character to ecumenism on January 29, 1959, when after letting the cardinals know of his intention to call a council, he added: "We entreat all of you to extend a renewed invitation to the faithful of the separated communities to follow Us amicably in this quest for unity and for grace, to which so many souls from all corners of the earth aspire." [14] The Council of the universal Church that John XXIII has in mind will busy itself not only with problems within the Catholic Church but also with the question of Christian discussion. Even before announcing the Council the Pope had indicated his concern for Church unity. His first radio address, given on October 29, 1958, the day after his election, already contained an appeal to the Eastern Church.[15] His 1958 Christmas message included an understanding reference to the "Orthodox Churches" of the Near East. The Pope expressed his regret over the persistence of the "vexing problem of the broken unity of the heritage of Christ." [16] The sadness of past defeats, he insisted, would not stop his efforts "to continue the loving invitation to Our separated brothers, who also carry on their forehead the name of Christ and who read His Holy Gospel and are not insensible to the inspirations of religious piety, and of a beneficent and blessed charity." [17] On January 18, 1959, alluding to the Octave of Prayer for Unity, he confided to the students of Capranica College in Rome that he was filled with anxiety "for those who, being within the Church do not hear the voice of God, for those who are separated but who bear the sign of the cross in their souls and their conduct, or in their solitude

---

[13] Message to the Clergy of Venice, April 23, 1959. *The Pope Speaks,* vol. 5, no. 3 (Summer, 1959), p. 297.

[14] *Ibid.,* vol. 5, no. 4 (Autumn, 1959), p. 401.

[15] *Ibid.,* vol. 5, no. 2 (Spring, 1959), p. 135.

[16] *Ibid.,* p. 131.

[17] *Ibid.*

seek the meaning of the Word of God in Sacred Scripture, for the multitudes who are still ignorant of the Redemption." [18]

The Holy Father has oftentimes come back to the idea of a Council. On March 15, 1959, he condemned all provincialism. The Church "is neither the Venetian nor the Milanese, nor the French, nor the Greek, nor the Slavic Church—to use the names of various nations—but the one apostolic and universal Church." [19] She has "neither divisions nor subdivisions." [20] On the contrary, "the principle of the unity of all the Churches among themselves is the sacred bond which insures the permanence of Christ's heritage over the centuries. We are all united with the first Apostle of our Lord according to the emblem engraved upon the episcopal seal of a great Bishop of the early Church: 'Fight together with Peter and reign together with Peter.' " [21] Speaking to the Federation of Catholic Universities on April 1, 1959, John XXIII thus described one aspect of the council: "It will not only afford a wonderful spectacle of the coherence, the unity, the harmony of the Holy Church of God, the city seated on a mountain, but, by its nature, will be an invitation to our separated brethren who bear the honored name of Christian, to return to the universal sheepfold, whose leadership and guardianship Christ entrusted to the most blessed Peter by an immutable decree." [22] On April 28th, on the occasion of the novena before the feast of Pentecost, John XXIII asked that "prostrate before the altar of the Virgin, who is rightfully called the Spouse of the Holy Spirit, We beg for the infusion of the gifts of the Paraclete, so that a new Pentecost might come to bring joy to the Christian family." [23]

Finally, on June 29, 1959, Pope John XXIII published his

---

[18] *D.C.*, February 15, 1959, n. 1297, col. 216.
[19] *The Pope Speaks,* vol. 5, no. 3 (Summer, 1959), p. 316.
[20] *Ibid.*
[21] *Ibid.*
[22] *Ibid.*, vol. 5, no. 4 (Autumn, 1959), p. 390.
[23] *D.C.*, May 10, 1959, n. 1303, col. 590.

first encyclical, *Ad Petri Cathedram*. This letter contains a long passage on unity. The Sovereign Pontiff described the admirable unity of the Catholic Church, which is a unity of faith, of government and of liturgical and sacramental practice. This unity nevertheless leaves a large margin to the individual initiative of theologians. The Pope adopted the ancient saying "Unity in what is necessary, freedom where there is doubt, charity in all." [24] John XXIII referred to the ecumenical movement. "We have taken note that almost all those who are adorned with the name of Christian, even though separated from Us and from one another, have sought to forge bonds of unity by means of many congresses and by establishing councils. This is evidence that they are moved by an intense desire for unity of some kind." [25] He also mentioned the catholicizing movements. "We are already aware, to Our great joy, that many of the communities that are separated from the See of Blessed Peter have recently shown some inclination toward the Catholic faith and its teachings. They have manifested a high regard for this Apostolic See and an esteem which grows greater from day to day as devotion to truth overcomes earlier misconceptions." [26]

Finally, addressing himself directly to separated Christians, the Pope launched an appeal for union. "We address, then, as brethren, all who are separated from Us . . . to all Our brethren and sons who are separated from the Chair of Blessed Peter, We say again: 'I am . . . Joseph, your brother.' Come, 'make room for us.' We want nothing else, pray God for nothing else but your salvation, your eternal happiness." [27] In preparation for the council John XXIII briefly outlined a program of spiritual ecumenism: "The outcome of the approaching Ecumenical Council will depend more on a crusade of fervent prayer than on human effort

---

[24] *D.C.*, July 19, 1959, n. 1308, col. 909.
[25] *The Pope Speaks*, vol. 5, no. 4 (Autumn, 1959), p. 369.
[26] *Ibid.*
[27] *Ibid.*, p. 373.

and diligent application. And so with loving heart We also invite to this crusade all who are not of this fold but reverence and worship God and strive in good faith to obey His commands." [28]

At this point we may draw our study of the development of ecumenism in the nineteenth and twentieth centuries to a close. The beginnings of the pontificate of John XXIII have given a new impetus to Catholic ecumenism. This official consecration crowns the encouragements that the Roman Pontiffs had already given it. Catholic ecumenism will surely become better known because of it, among Catholics as well as among other Christians. It may thereby gain apostles and find a large audience among theologians themselves.

Apart from this, the invitation to ecumenism formulated by Pope John XXIII will not be without influence on the direction taken by the ecumenical movement among the Orthodox as well as among Anglicans and Protestants. It is no longer possible to ignore the fact that the See of the Apostle Peter has adopted a friendly attitude towards Christians who are searching for the unity "for which Jesus Christ so ardently prayed to His Heavenly Father." [29]

The encyclical *Ad Petri Cathedram* marks the end of one period and the beginning of another.

---

[28] *Ibid.*, p. 372.
[29] *Ibid.*, p. 368.

CONCLUSION

Our study of the ecumenism of the past two centuries ends with a hope, the hope awakened by Pope John XXIII within the heart of ecumenical concern. This enduring, patient hope does not expect simple or quick solutions. As seen in the light of the long life of the Church, it is of no crucial importance whether she recovers from century-old schisms tomorrow afternoon or tomorrow evening. In the eyes of God, and to some extent in the eyes of the Church, "a thousand years are as a day." We must not give in to impatient discontent in these matters. To follow the slow rhythm that has providentially characterized the Church is to be very realistic and very humble.

Besides, it would be dangerous to put the desire for Christian unity on the level of politics. It must not devolve into a weapon for the defense of Christian civilization, and still less a bulwark of the Western way of life. Whether unity be viewed as both Catholicism and Orthodoxy see it, as the perfect gift of God to His Church, or as Protestantism considers it, as yet to come, it can only be a question of faith in and obedience to the Word of God. We must not think in terms of human reasoning, as if God's presence with His Church were in danger of extinction whenever ecumenical enterprises fail. Neither the official atheism of the Marxist regime, nor the practical agnosticism of the capitalist regime, or the political awakening of Islam or other non-Christian religions provide an acceptable argument in favour of ecumenism. It is born of an act of faith and hope, not of a reaction of fear. It can only develop along these same lines of faith and hope.

I will leave to my readers to decide for themselves what views they should take on the question of Christian unity and what corresponding conception they should form of the method and purpose of ecumenism. Catholics, Orthodox, Anglicans and Protestants will no doubt arrive at divergent positions. The nature of ecumenism is still largely open to theological discussion within Catholicism. It is not fitting that a book of mere history impose the author's conclusions on others. These conclusions are sufficiently indicated by the choice of historical material appearing in the chapters of this book. The author's conception of Catholic ecumenism and his estimation of Protestant ecumenism have already been stated in other works. Interested readers are at liberty to refer to them.

These pages ought to be closed, nonetheless, with an invitation to ecumenism. Let us therefore listen to what the late Cardinal Saliege, Archbishop of Toulouse, wrote in his pastoral letter of January, 1956:

"The more I reflect on the problem of Church unity, the more aware I am of the fact that the solution to this problem presumes a number of conditions:

1st. That the Churches keep a respectful silence in regard to one another.

2nd. That each Church know exactly what the doctrinal position of the others is.

3rd. That the members of each Church pray loyally and fervently for Church unity.

Christian truths are inter-related. People think too much about what divides us rather than about what we have in common. Under these conditions the solution to the problem is a long way off.

I know that this solution depends on the action of the Holy Spirit in our souls, yet, let this action be facilitated by good will.

I believe in the sincerity and value of the desire for unity. I believe in the value of and necessity for prayer to the end that this desire become efficacious." [1]

---

[1] *D.C.*, January 22, 1956, n. 1217, col. 97-8.